Friend,

Gentle Giant, full of grace,
You Bless Me!!

Blessings!

♡ Care

Book / Information
www.caretuk.com

Blog
www.carescorner.net

endorsements

"Loose Screws and Skinned Knees not only aptly describes Care's life, it illustrates a powerful truth. No matter how many times you fall down in life . . . no matter what challenge befalls you . . . there is always a way to put things back together and get going again. Care's words, like her life, embody The American Cancer Society's Relay For Life® motto: *Celebrate! Remember! Fight Back!* ever hoping that you, too, will remember to *Celebrate! Remember! Fight Back!*"

- *Sarah Robinson, District Executive Director*
  American Cancer Society, Great West Division, Inc.

"It happens to everyone. One minute you're skipping along; the next you're staring into the gaping jaws of suffering. When physical hardship hits you broadside—such as happened with Care Tuk—you find yourself searching for a hold . . . something to keep you sane and keep you up. Care has found that hand-hold in the Word of God and, despite years of surgeries and rehab, she has maintained a smile sent straight from heaven. Her sense of humor underscores that the joy of the Lord is definitely her strength. If you're looking for someone who might identify with your struggles, Care is the one. And her new book is her personal encouragement just for you!"

- *Joni Eareckson Tada*
  JAF International Disability Center

"Eleven bouts with cancer. A tragic car accident. Ninety plus surgeries. Yet she will have you laughing with her and believing you too can conquer life's struggles! Care's stories demonstrate a simple, witty, practical, positive, and inspiring faith—providing fresh insight into the power of persistence, optimism, positive attitude, resilience and humor. You will laugh. You will cry. You will be challenged and empowered to overcome any obstacle that faces you in life! This is a must-read book of hope."

- *Dan Miller, Author*
  Living, Laughing & Loving Life!

"Normally, you wouldn't use the words "fortitude" and "fun" to describe the same person, but Care Tuk is no normal person! She has faced trials that would have put the rest of us flat on our backs. For Care, each trail is just another mountain to climb—joyfully, compellingly, willingly . . . humorously—praising her Lord with each step. She has lived her life as a living testimony of how God sustains. The stories are real and the storyteller is truly the "real deal." Be blessed and spurred on by these words from Care. You're going to find yourself with a lot less whining in your life and a lot more winning!"

- *Carole Inman*
  AnGeL Ministries

loose screws & skinned knees

turning life's obstacles and adversity into opportunities and adventure

loose screws &skinned knees

turning life's obstacles and adversity into opportunities and adventure

care tuk

Photography by Colin Tyler Bogucki.
Graphic Design by Curt Sell.

ISBN: 978-0-615-42913-7

Printed in the United States of America

Babe:
Forever + + + . . .
Thanks for believing in me
and
reminding me often how much you love me.
Ummers!
Lady

contents

acknowledgements

Forever Grateful . . .

My story could never have been put to print without a team of people who believed in me enough to see it through. There is definitely no "I" on this team! Through thick and thin, richer or poorer, sickness and health, and at times almost until death did us part, this team has been nothing short of God's miraculous handiwork at its best.

I'll forever be grateful to my loving husband Bill who wouldn't let me give up on this life-long dream. He chose me to be his Lady, his wife, the mother to his kids, but most of all, his best friend, with God's help. Equal gratitude goes to Jamie and Tim, our incredible kids, who dubbed us "Toys R Us" parents. (We don't want to grow up.) They also remind me that I've embarrassed them enough over their lifetimes, so this book will be just fine.

A true Godcidence is the only fitting definition for Jay Fordice and Don Woodward. Whodda thunk that the son and grandson of my mom's best friend from middle school would become my praying, printing, and web publishing partners? May your countless hours of hard work and infinite wisdom be blessed a hundredfold.

A shout out has to go to the incredible "behind the scene team" that Jay put together. I hope someday I will get to meet you—whether here, there, or in the air!

To my Heroes of Hope—you know who you are! To my family and friends near and far. To my colleagues, my community connects, and the myriad of medical people who have placed the band-aids, tightened loose screws, or pulled me together with fishing line. You have each had a huge impact on helping make sure that the adversities and obstacles I have faced turned into adventures and opportunities. Thank you for journeying with me, encouraging me, praying with me and for me, and always making memories everywhere we have travelled!

To Dan and Juju, my gratitude for passing the torch. Remember you have never retired, you just get tired. (That's what you get for being dream-makers!)

To Joni and Ken Tada—need I say more? Comrades, cohorts, and champions. *Oh, what a fellowship. Oh, what a joy divine.* Thanks for letting me tag along with you, and thank you for teaching me that *it's not in trying but in trusting; it's not in running, but in resting; it's not in wondering but in praying that we find the strength of the Lord.*

The memory of those who have gone before me looms large. Parents, loved ones, teachers, and friends. Their love planted the seeds for this book. Their life lessons spurred me to grow. I'm glad my lifetime is forever and that forever is a lifetime. For that, I am truly blessed. I know I am in Good Hands. (And yes, Dad, I know it's not Allstate!) What great hands to be in to tighten my loose screws and to love on my skinned knees!

Seeking first . . . one day at a time!

loose screws & skinned knees

turning life's obstacles and adversity into opportunities and adventure

preface

For years people have said to me, "You should write a book!"

Doubting I had anything people would want to hear, I started asking them, "What should I say? What do you want to hear?"

Time and time again they replied: "Tell us how you do it. People won't believe all that you have been through."

They would approach me after a speaking engagement and tell me: "Show us life is real and not a tall tale! Tell us how you have made it through all your adversities and yet turned them into adventures."

After hearing my story, they would challenge me: "Tell us how you have kept your perspective through cancer, drunken driving accidents, and the challenge of raising special needs kids. Tell us how, when you faced seemingly insurmountable obstacles, you turned them around into unbelievable opportunities."

So, for all who have sojourned with me, dreamed with me, prayed with and for me—for those who have believed one more time and who want to venture on some surreal adventures— come along. This is my story of faith triumphing over fear.

Turn the pages. Shuffle through them. Flip back and forth. Come and go as you please. This is not a "how-to" book or "fix-it" manual. Rather, this is a collection of nuggets, mined through tough times and trials, joys and celebrations . . . all in the daily grind we call life.

This is *my* life.

introduction

It was minus ten degrees outside. An angry arctic wind howled through the vents and open spaces of the room, twisting around each corner. With each large, glacial gust, the windows shook and rattled. I wrapped my polar fleece tighter around me and hugged closer to my husband next to me. I shivered with cold, as much as fear, as a draft followed the solid swift knock that swung the door open.

In walked Dr. Larry.

Not many people, much less a doctor, can carry off wearing a Hawaiian shirt, jeans, and flip flops—especially on a blustery, below-zero, frigid Alaskan day! Then again, in the five years I had known Larry, I had never seen him without his signature attire accompanied by his contagious, positive, and lively disposition.

Living in a relatively rural area in Alaska, it's hard not to have personal and professional lives cross. Besides being doctor/patient, Larry and I were colleagues. His role was as an oncologist, medical mentor and friend to many. My role, for many years, had been spent as a rural occupational therapist, ambassador for the American Cancer Society, and community leader.

Our mischievous mannerisms and upbeat attitudes punctuated our actions and conversations. We often found ourselves straying off point. Our encounters, while not always about pleasant subjects (aka: cancer), had always been positive.

But this time was different. This time *he* was different.

3

He plopped down on his circular stool and rolled up close to the leather chair I was sitting in. He put his hands on my knees and looked me square in the eyes. Then he looked over to my husband as tears welled up in his eyes. The room went silent. My husband unsuccessfully tried to hide the tear trickling down his own cheek.

I had come to pride myself over the years on the idea that nothing could faze me or surprise me. But again? *Really?*

Larry broke the icy silence, accompanied by another blast of arctic air and ice pellets hitting the window, "Well guys, how are we going to do this?"

We had already been given the news, confirming the fact we had known for months. The lump I had been feeling off to the side my stomach was a tumor. It was cancer. After several medical missed cues and round-abouts due to my complex case, we pushed to have my records sent to the surgeon for further exploration.

Several weeks later, surgery confirmed it. It wasn't rocket science, but it didn't make the news any easier to digest. Rather, it made me angrier at myself for not pushing harder—not demanding more. And now, staring us right in the face, was cancer number eleven. Colon cancer, stage three. Our options were limited.

"Well guys, how are we going to do this?" Larry's words rang in my ear.

I have been fighting cancer ever since the age of sixteen. First in my mom's life, losing her battle to colon cancer when I was just a junior in high school. Then, at the age of nineteen, I received my own diagnosis of cancer. The first of many.

Up until this morning, I had beaten it. I had fought it, and won, ten other times. Cervical cancer. Uterine cancer. Ovarian cancer. Thyroid cancer. Lymph cancer. Stomach cancer. Breast cancer, twice. And two struggles with malignant melanomas. Now this. Number eleven. Ninety-four surgeries (not all from cancer) later and we were facing it all over again.

Most of my cancers have been a result of my mom's use of the drug DES while she was pregnant with me. It wasn't her fault. She was doing what she thought was best. You see, my mother had difficulty carrying babies to full term. Her doctor prescribed a drug that was being used in the late 1940s and early 1950s to prevent miscarriages. It was called diethylstilbestrol, or DES, and it seemed to work wonders.

While DES proved to prevent miscarriages, it remained to be seen what else it would do. The drug was too new to know of any long-term side effects associated with it. And lucky me, I would be part of the first generation of side-effect finders.

And findings we found.

My due date was October 30, 1954. I was born September 8—more than seven weeks premature. Weighing in at a mere three and a half pounds, I spent four weeks in an incubator. Four weeks until my parents could even hold me. But I fought, and I survived.

Now I was staring Dr. Larry in the face wondering how to even process his question:

Well guys, how are we going to do this?

The physical side effects and hazards left from the DES continue to plague me today—more than 55 years later.

Degenerative joint disease. Infertility. Poor immune system. Chronic fatigue. Epstein-Barr. They all have become trademarks of the DES aftermath—unwelcomed issues I deal with on a daily basis.

If my life wasn't interesting enough, a near-fatal car accident in 1984 added to my pain, leaving me broken and battered. Thanks to a careless drunk driver—hitting my stopped car—my face was smashed in, my arm and torso were severely torn, and my shoulders were destroyed.

The police estimate the drunk driver was going 50 miles per hour when he hit me. It was 10:30 in the morning. My face had to be rebuilt and my shoulders pinned together by fishing line and anchor bolts. My back was fused and screwed together in four places. But I survived, against the odds, and continued on in this battle called life.

And now . . . cancer . . . again.

Well guys, how are we going to do this?

No question I have learned how to fight over the years. It had become my calling of sorts. Like in 2001, when a brain bleed of an unknown origin left me in physical, occupational, and speech therapy for more than 28 months. The doctors had to do a craniotomy, carving out a square of my skull, then screwing and bolting me back together with a permanent "J" tattoo.

I had to learn how to walk, talk and even feed myself all over again—all in the midst of the 9-11 terrorist attack mayhem. (Try expressing your emotion and concern for family and friends who lived in New York City with no ability to share it with the world.) The brain bleed had its own terrorist-type effect on my body, leaving me with weakness, poor coordination, and uneven balance even to this day.

And now . . . cancer . . . again.

Well guys, how are we going to do this?

The DES that my mom took, giving me a chance at life, put more than a few orthopedic surgeons' kids through college. Due to the degenerative joint disease, the orthopedic office at the hospital had to put in a revolving door for me. And I've kept them busy for generations.

The surgeon who is currently responsible for keeping my screws tight and my walk upright is the son of the surgeon who first worked on me in 1971. The son's claim to fame on my broken body, beside two "regular" knee replacements, includes a state of the art upper and lower leg rod and a mechanical piston action knee. (Yes, I am The Bionic Woman).

But really? Cancer? Again?

How many times do I have to beat the odds? And really . . .

How are we going to do this?

How have my husband and I faced both sets of parents dying at an early age? How did we face losing all four of them to cancer or heart disease? How have we faced adopting a daughter with special needs, the product of a teen pregnancy? (We recently found out she had a life threatening congenital heart defect due to the young pregnancy.)

How did we handle living in the "red zone" of Mount St. Helens as it blew its top in 1980? How did we handle the thrill of being given the opportunity of our life dream—working on the foreign medical and construction field—only to have it ripped away after being hit by the drunk driver? How did we handle a house fire? How did we handle living through four (or is it five?) floods?

How did we handle adopting and raising a son who had been severely abused and neglected, leaving him with autistic tendencies and mild cerebral palsy? He was just learning how to walk and talk when we adopted him at age five. He didn't know what a tricycle was. He had never seen Legos. The only toy he had when he joined our family was a stuffed ALF his foster parents had given him, at his first-ever birthday party. How would we see him into adulthood successfully? How would we walk the social, emotional, and medical maze with him?

How did we do it?

And how . . . Lord, how are we going to do this . . . again?

I sat in the leather chair, broken. Here I was, an ambassador for the American Cancer Society. I touted early detection. I had beaten cancer ten times before! Yet, here I sat, watching tears brim in Dr. Larry's eyes and quietly slip down my husband's cheek. I felt sucker-punched, somehow betrayed. The fear that gripped my very being was like the ice that pelted the windows. I felt tossed and beaten like the bitter arctic air that howled through the walls. And the question echoed in my head . . .

Well guys, how are we going to do this?

There were no other options. We were going to do this the same way we have done everything else: hit it straight on with head held high — taking it one day at a time. We would take the obstacle—we would take the adversity—and look for the adventure and the opportunities.

Oh, the places we would go because of the adversities! Russia, Albania, Ghana, Tobago, and the West Indies. We would not have been around the world reaching out to others affected by disability had we not walked the road ourselves. We would not know how to relate to a mother with a child with cerebral palsy had we not been through the same struggles. It didn't matter the language barriers. The heart speaks the same language everywhere. We would have the chance to bring these people hope and to offer them a future.

But how?

By sharing the odd, yet powerful reality that life's obstacles and adversities truly do give you opportunities and adventures. They let you spread your wings. They let you experience life. And they let you—as crazy as it may sound—experience the true freedom of brokenness and dependence.

It's the little things in life that will get us through the storms. Sitting down at Care's Corner, after running away a time or three. Returning to our hot cocoa and our quiet times. Listening to the still, small voice that guides us and leads us and fills us. Sitting by the river and finding that there is peace. Looking up to the mountains and seeing all that is and all that can be. Knowing that even if we are sentenced to pain, we will never do it alone.

We may skin some knees along the way. We may need a few shiny screws to hold our broken bodies together. But our feet have wings and our hearts are full of hope. And best of all, our Savior is ready and waiting to pick us up and set us straight again . . . and again . . . and again.

How will we do it? Straight on and head held high, taking it one day at a time.

That's how we will do it.

1

they call me care

I love it when people ask for my name. A quizzical look normally comes over their face, as if to say, "Are you pulling my leg? That can't *really* be."

When a person asks me over the phone, I find it especially amusing. It normally goes something like this:

"May I have your name please?"

"Sure! It's Care Tuk."

"And your name?"

"That is my name. Care Tuk."

"So, that's your company name?"

"No, that's *my* name."

"Oh." (Silence.) "Wait. Can I get your first name please?"

"Care."

"You're sure that's your first name and not your company name?"

"Yes, ma'am, I'm sure that's my first name."

"Well then, ma'am, how do you spell that? Is it C-A-R?"

This is when my eyes begin to roll upwards and my teeth begin to clench tightly. I so badly want to respond with something like, *And what does c-a-r spell for you?* Yet I refrain

11

and politely respond, "No, it is C-A-R-E. You know, like Care Bear. Care package. Who cares?"

That's when we both begin to chuckle a bit. But sadly, I know all too well the direction this conversation is going. I prepare myself.

"Now, Care," they respond. "That is your first name, right?"

"Right."

"So then, Care, what is your last name?"

"Tuk. T as in Turtle, U as in Unicorn, and K as in King."

"Okay. That's T-U-C-K, correct?"

"Not quite. Leave out the "C." Just Tuk. T-U-K."

There is silence once again on the other end. I can almost hear their brain working overtime. I wait for it to sink in.

"Care Tuk? *Really?*"

"Yep!"

"Well, that *is* an unusual name."

"Lady," I respond, "you don't know the half of it!"

I haven't always gone by Care Tuk. I was born Carolyn Jane. That's right, plain ol' Jane. I grew up where the bluest skies are supposedly found (according to Perry Como's song), and where nights are sleepless (according to Meg Ryan and Tom Hanks). Seattle, Washington.

I was actually raised in an area known as the Eastside. My parents were middle school buddies, high school sweethearts, and were married after each of them finished their service to our country. My dad was in the Coast Guard and my mother served in the Navy.

My parents were a proud portion of the people who hammered and nailed homes together in the early 1950s. They helped develop what is now the prosperous suburb known as Mercer Island. I give away my age when I say I remember when the I-90 toll bridge cost only a dime (it has since been replaced) and when Bellevue Square really was just a square (it is now an expansive mall).

My dad loomed at a towering 6 foot, 5 inches tall. His twinkling blue eyes revealed a sense of humor enjoyed by all. People who knew him tell me he never said an unkind word about anyone. A rare quality to be sure.

Providing for a family of six, he labored long and hard for the local telephone company, affectionately known at the time as "Ma Bell." My dad was in charge of construction and upkeep of several of the lines and towers in our surrounding area including Renton, Kent, Auburn, Enumclaw, and Issaquah. Back then it was sprawling farmland and hills. Not the case today.

His leadership was pivotal in the recovery of communication after the 1962 Columbus Day Storm that carried winds of 170+ miles per hour, wreaking havoc up and down the Washington and Oregon coastlines. In his later years with the phone company he was head of safety, and was responsible for key legislation throughout the region.

But more importantly, he was a great father and husband; loving my mom and protecting and challenging each one of us kids every step of the way. He was the one who gave me my life verse. He was the one who directed our little clan. He was the one who pointed us upward.

I still remember him as the fun-loving father, the substitute Sunday school teacher (with his paper airplane flying contest

– so spiritual), and the wise leader with powerful words of wisdom at just the right time. And my mom? She was just the right match for him.

I grew up in the "Leave it to Beaver" era where we were fortunate to have a stay-at-home mom. That was until the economy changed in the late 1960s and she returned to work at our local high school.

I don't think I fully appreciated her role at home until I was a working mom myself. There's nothing like the gift of being able to have a mom home to greet you as you jump off the school bus, or the countless hours she spent helping with Camp Fire Girls, or the leisure of having friends over during lazy afternoons.

My childhood consisted of neighborhoods and lemonade stands, ladies bowling leagues and bridge clubs, where "mom's rules reigned" unless it was "wait until your father gets home." We never failed to quiver at those words, especially when her deep brown eyes pointed down her long slender nose. Mom was definitely the disciplinarian, but it was Dad's large footsteps that would make us shake!

Mom taught me how to set priorities and how to know my limits. How blessed I was to have parents who believed in their wedding vows and their promises to each other—an example I feel blessed to share in my own life today.

I was born number three of four kids. My parents struggled with miscarriages after having my oldest sister. The struggles would lead to my mom participating in a new drug regime called diethylstilbestrol, or DES for short. For those who know it, they know the bad comes with the good. While it did help with the miscarriages, it didn't prepare them for some of the side effects that they, and we, would experience later in life.

With my oldest sister nine years my senior, I often thought of her as a second mother of sorts. When my parents weren't home, *her* rules reigned. But her chocolate chip cookies reigned even more supreme! By the time I was in middle school she was in college.

As a treat, my parents would put me on a Greyhound bus where I would sit in the front seat next to the driver and travel alone (all of 40 miles) to Tacoma to visit my sister. I would spend a weekend submerged in the antics of college and sorority life. We would go on walks to the soda fountain, eat at the cafeteria, and stay up late. To this day I can remember one of my sister's friends, now a colleague of mine, who went screaming down the hall after cutting her leg shaving. It took me years for my friends to convince me to shave my legs when it came time!

It wasn't until my own college years when I really got to know my oldest sister. She and her husband lived in the same town as me. As they began to raise their family, I had the privilege and joy of seeing them do life. Sisters we were, and close friends we became.

My brother was number two in line. Even though I was still the "pesky little sister," he always looked out for me. I envied much of what he got to do, especially with athletics and outdoor adventures. I tended to be somewhat of a tom-boy growing up and had little interest in the girlie-girl things. My brother's activities and antics always proved to be more intriguing and exciting, and when I was lucky, I got to tag along.

I learned a lot by watching my big brother. He never gave up on his dreams. His fortitude and ferocious hard work, no matter the adversity, have always been the backbone of his accomplishments. He has designed, developed, and implemented one of the most successful businesses for recycling land debris in the state of Washington.

His company, North Mason Fiber, is the only permitted facility on the Olympic Peninsula to produce their own, state-of-the-art, truly organic compost. It is sold nationally, as well as internationally. His forward thinking and fastidious hard work will leave its mark for generations to come. And I get to say: "That's *my* big brother!"

My youngest sister was the closest in age to me. We were only 16 months apart. And like many siblings, we were close, living and playing together for hours on end. We shared a room and many of our toys. Our parents often treated us like twins, even dressing us alike when we were little.

But twins we are not! I wish I could say I had the class to pull off her attractive feminine look or navigate the Eastside traffic with such grace. Me? I'm the casual athletic Alaska type. Moose are my only road hazards and my attire of choice consists of cargo pants and hooded sweatshirts.

Living in the sleepy suburb of Mercer Island, I enjoyed the neighborhood existence and the safety that those days brought. And that's where I met Kate, my best friend (or in today's context – BFF). Even to this day I consider her my closest of friends.

Growing up, Kate and I hardly knew what would happen past the end of the day, much less the years that would lie ahead. We would spend hours on our tin-can-and-string telephone, strung between our houses. Convinced our invention worked, we would shout to each other late into the night, and often into the wee hours of the morning.

As we look back, some 50 years later, we giggle thinking what our fathers must have thought. They both worked for the local telephone company. They both could hear us shouting. There were more than several nights that we would get in big trouble, mainly after waking our families (and neighbors) with our boisterous talking into the tin can phone.

Kate also had a chicken named Myrtle. She was a little, extremely ornery, black Banty hen. Myrtle had a two story 'condo' chicken house. (She was the envy of all the other hens on the block.) Downstairs were her 'living quarters' where her food, water, scratch, and oyster shells stayed. Upstairs were her roost and bedroom. The care for Myrtle was totally my friend's responsibility, unless they were on vacation. That's when the 'honor' was bestowed upon me.

Kate and I would spend hours with Myrtle. We would talk with her. We would let her out of her condo to walk in the grass and scratch in the dirt. We would let her roam as we played with our plastic thoroughbred and palomino ponies. In our minds, we were country girls, living on the farm. And on more than one occasion it would take the booming voice of Kate's mother to bring us back to our cultured neighborhood in our Seattle suburb.

"Now girls," she would remind us, "don't forget you have to do your chores and clean up after Myrtle before you can get back to goofing off."

Goofing off? We were planning our futures as farm girls! How could that be goofing off? You could hear our groans from Seattle to Mt. Rainier. But we knew there was no use in protesting. Gathering up our horses we were off to 'scoop up' after Myrtle.

Oh, the tragic life.

Summertime would bring vacations to the ocean, trips to Hood Canal, and lazy days reading and playing outside. And as always, we never missed the famed "camp out" on the Fourth of July. It was what we lived for.

Pitching our pup tent in the vacant lot near our house, Kate and I would count the stars through the small screened windows until slumber overtook us. And never fail, at the crack of dawn, my father would poke his head in and start singing. He was accompanied by John Philip Sousa's *Stars and Stripes Forever* blaring loud enough the ground would thump and shake.

"Be kind to your web-footed friend, for a duck may be some-body's mother!" he would boom in his baritone voice.

We wouldn't dare admit it, but it was pretty funny. This six-foot-five giant poking his head into a dinky pup tent and singing at the top of his lungs! The rightful beginning to a special day, filled with baseball games, Frisbee toss, and wonderful BBQ with my dad's amazing potato salad. All passing the time—leading the way for the fireworks to come.

Ahhh . . . my life as a kid was good.

2
tall tales

And then, of course, there was my extended family. People like Grandpa Harry, Aunt Ruth and Aunt Betty. If I close my eyes and breathe in real deep, I can still smell Grandpa Harry's Cuban cigars. While I am a staunch advocate against smoking, especially since Grandpa's only son, my father, died of lung and metastasized kidney cancer, I will always love the smell of Grandpa's old stogies. He could entertain us for hours with cigar smoke circles and stories.

Grandpa Harry stayed in an assisted living facility smack dab overlooking Pike Place Market and Elliot Bay. He could watch the local ferries come and go, or listen to their mournful horns sound when fog shrouded the twelve stories below him. With each visit he would take us on "the tour" introducing us to "the ladies" (the nuns who ran the facility). We had met each one on previous visits, but he would still tout our accomplishments of years gone by.

If it wasn't time with Grandpa Harry, it was the highly anticipated, over-night stay with my Great Aunt Ruth. With her ever coiffed silver-gray hair, her arthritic kinked pinky that made her look like she was drinking her tea with the Queen

Mum, and always dressed to the nines, she would open her city house once a year for an over-night stay prior to *Breakfast with Santa* – a famed family tradition.

Oh, how I loved playing with her numerous recue cats that roamed her turn-of-the-century home. And bath time was always a pleasure as I squealed with delight, splashing water in the deep, cavernous, antique claw-foot bathtub. Once scrubbed and polished, I would proudly walk across the street to Holy Names Academy/Convent, where Aunt Ruth's daughter, our cousin Patricia, lived. (We called her Pish for short.) Her new name as a nun was Sister Mary Ruth Ellen – which always confused me. Why take a new name as a grown-up?

Sister Pish always wore a long black skirt, a starched black and white habit, and a crucifix that seemed to hang to her knees. Hanging on a silver linked chain was a pair of sharp long-nosed scissors. I dared not ask for what! I was scared to death to move off the high back silk fabric parlor chair that I had been boosted up to sit on.

I still remember pleading with Aunt Ruth on many occasions to "puleeze" let me leave the hallowed 'visiting parlor' and have Sister Pish escort me to the ladies restroom. I'm not sure I ever really had to use the facilities. I just wanted to hear my patent leather shoes echo down the long oak corridor, occasionally hitting a board that would eerily squeak.

As I walked I tried to envision what must be under each nun's habit and wondered (to myself, of course) if God had taken their hair away too when they took their vow of nunnery? Today, Pish is a modern nun wearing regular street clothes. To this day, I've never had the nerve to ask her what was under those habits!

The overnight adventure with Great Aunt Ruth would always conclude with our annual trek to *Breakfast with Santa*. Aunt Ruth always made sure I was dressed as smartly as she was. Every hair was in place. White gloves on my little hands.

I still remember one specific occasion. We were on our way to the big event when we heard an ambulance siren in the air. Aunt Ruth pulled over and quickly turned to me in the back seat: "Care, bow your head and close your eyes."

My eyes popped wide with wonder, but I was quick to obey.

"Precious Lord Jesus, protect whoever will be riding in the ambulance. Be with all the people involved—the drivers, the policemen, the doctors, and nurses. But especially be with the family, for I ask this in the name of the Father, Son and Holy Ghost, Amen."

As quickly as she pulled over, she pulled back on the road and we were off.

I'll never forget our wonderful *Breakfasts with Santa*, all dressed and coiffed. And I'll always remember those times at the convent to visit Cousin Pish as well. But the memory that has stuck with me all these years is the power of prayer, every time I hear a siren. Whether it is a fire truck, a police car, or an ambulance, as I pull over I pray. For I learned on that day the importance of chasing an ambulance with prayer. You never know who may be in it. Someday, it just may be you.

It was not just family that made my life special growing up. It was close family friends as well. One family in particular—the Hawes clan—was truly instrumental in my young life.

For all I knew, my parents had known them since the beginning of time. Not only did they attend the same church, but the adults all played in a regular bridge club together. They had three sons who were close in age to my older brother and sister.

This family was very tall in stature. Not just your usual tall. But tall, tall! The mother was somewhere around six feet, before the ravages of osteoporosis hit her. The father stood around six foot, seven inches. The sons stood taller than dad, which made it a good thing that their ceilings were the high Victorian ones.

And let's just say, when I visited, I felt like I was in the land of the giants, especially in my younger years. Even though I have grown to 5'9", I still feel like I'm in the land of the giants when I see them!

Growing up, I remember my brother spending hours at their place on the lake, playing hoops, water skiing, fishing, and just hanging out. Heaven forbid if I even tried to sneak up the stairs to the "lair" from which the elusive laughter emanated. That is where the comic books were traded and who knows what else.

I remember trying every trick in my limited 'younger sister book' to get on the inside of their little pack. How I tried to get my brother to let me tag along as he packed up his tackle box and pole, choosing the walking trek on those magical early summer mornings. You know the kind – the ones where the dew is still fresh on the blades of manicured suburb Seattle lawns, the sun beginning to rise over the Cascades, and the slight chill in the early-morning air. I remember being especially envious when he went off to catch an elusive fish or three, and not wanting a little twit sister to get in his way.

Now that I'm writing, maybe it wasn't that he didn't want

me there, but maybe it was that he wanted some of the sweet solitude of those summer mornings . . . alone. In my defense, it was their fault that they taught me how to fish . . . or showed me the best place to snag a little perch . . . or passed on the secret skills of water-skiing on one ski!

I idolized my brother and his friends. They were fun. They were funny. They were talented. And on top of it all, they would—usually—put up with me.

I loved visiting the Hawes' house. With my love for swimming, it was my heaven. Set on a lake, they had a wonderfully spacious yard with a perennial croquet set ready for players. Uncle K, as I called the dad, kept an impeccable small apple orchard and amazing rhododendrons that greeted you as you opened their creaky faded white gate. His geranium pots on the back porch could have easily graced any *Better Homes and Garden* magazine issue.

On one of my rare overnight stays, he swore me to secrecy as I begged for the bazillionth time of how he grew such huge geraniums. It wasn't until years later that he admitted to buffaloing me – that his secret about growing was on the back of the geranium fertilizer box, and it wasn't fish fertilizer on the first Friday and Miracle Gro water on Mondays. (Talk about gullible little girls.)

Besides being fooled by giant gentlemen, one of the memories that is inscribed not just in my brain, but in my heart, is when I would be invited to "help" Mrs. Hawes. Not having any other women in her home, and living among the living large, I would occasionally be bestowed the honor of coming down to spend the day. I would help in the morning, then spend the afternoon either helping with other "woman's work" or, if the weather cooperated, I'd get to engage in my passion—swimming. If I was *totally* lucky, and the guys were *totally* bored, they might even invite me for a round of water-skiing.

I still remember the tasks. The "help" was normally making chocolate-chip cookies for the giants in the house. Considering who lived there, it was no simple task. A half dozen cookies would fit in the palm of the boy's hands. And, if I'm not mistaken, the Good Lord graced us with two!

Cookie making usually meant a quadruple batch. To this day, long after my own kids are grown, it is hard *not* to make at least a double and sometimes, I kid you not, a quadruple batch! (Thank goodness for freezers.)

Being all of nine years old, I can remember more than once stifling back alligator tears as the boys and their buddies would fly through the kitchen and scoop up the cookies. They would literally take every cookie that I had just spent three hours making – a half dozen cookies in each hand.

As soon as they would leave the kitchen and head to their lair, I'd let a tear or two trickle into the mix, and start all over. At that, Mrs. Hawes would simply come over, give me a hug, and with a twinkle in her eye say, "Welcome to my world, little one!"

I would look up in awe and wonder just how she did it. In her later years, she and I would spend hours together. I would visit her when she was in an assisted living complex, and then later when she moved into a nursing home. She struggled as she pondered why God was letting her live out her later years in ravaging pain and decreasing size.

We came to the conclusion that her 'assignment' in life was not just to be one of my "other mothers," but it was to raise boys who would play in the NBA and love chocolate chip cookies.

Even more, her assignment was to be a prayer warrior, and that job wasn't done. She would continue to make sure that her tear-streaked cheeks would grow the boys into men. They would become men of integrity, men of honor, men others would look up to, not just literally, but figuratively.

These men would be men who would raise children who would continue the tradition of honor, integrity, skill, and talent. They would become men who would honor their mother's memory (and mine) by the men they had become, the basketball they would play, and the cookies they loved.

For the most part, my life as a child wasn't much different from most other kids. My time would come. My trials were just around the bend. But at that time, in my little safe-haven of Mercer Island, all was good and right and perfect.

3

this roller coaster called life

I learned at an early age that you can make it through anything if you have faith, family, friends, and fun. But sometimes I took the latter a bit too far.

Growing up, the name Carolyn Jane was used *only* if I was in serious trouble, or, with a crescendo tone, if my parent's point needed strong emphasis. Like the time I broke the rules about going into my best friend Kate's house before school.

The rules were clear:

- Don't dawdle on your way to the bus stop in the morning.
- Don't go into Kate's house when no parents were home.

But what's a child to do?

Our parents would most likely never have found out that I broke the cardinal rules except for one tiny detail—the 1965 Seattle Earthquake.

As the 6.5 magnitude earthquake rumbled and roared, I screamed at the top of my lungs. I thought that the entire wrath of God was upon me because I had broken the rules and entered my best friend's laundry room to play with a toy as I waited for her to come out and catch the school bus. I dropped the toy truck and went crying and screaming out into the driveway as it rippled in ribbons along with the quake.

With sighs of relief and tears streaming down our faces, we heard my mother call from three homes away. As she held us in her solid embrace, we blurted out what we were doing when the earthquake had hit. As soon as it popped out of my mouth, I knew that I would be hearing the name Carolyn Jane.

Or there was the time I snuck into the school gym during lunch time, on a dare, and climbed the cargo net that hung from the high ceiling to the floor. I was doing fine. I even made it to the top and had climbed over to the cheers of the gathering crowd.

I would have been free and clear, had my foot not gotten caught in a coil of cargo rope. As I tried to pull myself free I went down on my outstretched hand. I did everything I could to keep from crying, acting like it was no big deal. The only problem was, I couldn't turn my hand over, and soon it had swollen to the size of a grapefruit. It was a little hard to hide from my teacher, who then found out what really happened out at recess.

It seemed like an eternity waiting for my mom to come pick me up and take me to the doctor. That's where we found out I had a fractured hand and wrist. While I did have a great badge of courage—disobedient, but peer approved—I sure heard the words Carolyn Jane used a lot the six weeks I was in the cast.

So, yes, Carolyn Jane was clearly used for discipline. But the name Care was a term of endearment used by my family and close friends. I embraced the name, and as I stretched my individual teenage wings, I introduced myself only as Care.

To this day, I rarely answer to Carolyn. And since high

school, it has been the only name I have gone by. When people ask me if Care is my given name, I always answer, "Yes." For, in all sincerity, the name was given to me. It was just used for those special occasions when I decided not to directly disobey my parents.

Now, don't get me wrong. I wasn't the only one of the kids who could get into trouble. Isn't that what brothers are for?

I can't even begin to imagine what it was like growing up with three sisters – one older, two younger. One versus three. Even I know that those aren't great odds! Can you imagine the wait time for the bathroom? Yet, sometimes those odds can work in your favor.

While I was getting myself into trouble, my brother was—in my mind—getting the royal treatment. Like . . . why does *he* get the horned-toads in his room and I can't? Or, why does *he* get an aquarium, with *real* angel fish and plecostomus? And me? I get one goldfish with magic rocks that crust over in less than a week. (And the rocks outlasted the goldfish by three days!)

How come *he* gets a room to himself? How come *he* gets to play drums? How come I'm stuck with stupid piano lessons?

Oh, how I wished I could have been his twin brother when I was younger. I was so jealous of his tickets to adventure—scuba diving, camp on Orcas Island (after selling a bazillion cans of honey peanuts) or playing basketball with future NBA players. I would longingly look out the window as he would take his coveted basketball over to the hoop on the telephone pole and shoot for hours on end.

It would be a golden day for me when he would allow me to lose at a game of Horse. I could tell how much he *really* minded when it changed to a game of Pig! I would drift off to sleep with his stories about spear-fishing and underwater construction, never aware of the real dangers he faced.

It would be several years later when I would finally have my own opportunity to scuba dive. I can still remember my first night dive. I was taken back to the times when my brother would narrate what I thought were just tall tales. Tales of tight scuba gear, his sun bleached hair and sun scorched nose, his eyes twinkling bluer than I had ever seen them.

His tales had been spiked with "oh, wow!" and "the fish were huge!" The stories were locked away in his private notebook, padlocked shut, safe from snooping sisters. But every once in a while, he let me in on his wonderful world, written down in the notebook he called Fairy Tales.

I still remember gliding in silence in the cold, dark waters beside the ferry dock jetty, soaking up the flashlight view of wolf eels and octopus, ling cod and hermit crabs. I realized I had been given my 'big brother' dream at long last! Oh, how I wished he could see me!

It finally made sense. Diving was his ticket to peace—complete freedom and silence, wonder and excitement. His terms. His excitement. His time to escape and breathe and dream of what lay ahead—no fairy tales, just wonderful plans for the future.

I look to where my brother is today. He's a successful international businessman who took his dreams, his excitement, his quiet wonder, and built a company that is cutting edge. Fairy tales? I think not. I think hard work and dreams realized.

While my brother was out looking for adventure, it seemed adventure came looking for my sisters and me, too, on occasion. We didn't have to go far to make a little bit of drama of our own.

Growing up, there never was a dull moment in our house. Sometimes that was a good thing. But sometimes, sadly, it was not. Like the time I still remember with just one violent word— CRRRACK!

I remember the day as if it were yesterday. Excitement swirled about the air. I knew something special would be happening as my mother had taken out the lace tablecloth. I was given the honor of polishing the good silver and making sure the good china and crystal goblets were bright and clean. The silver candle sticks with long white taper candles were being brought out as well. I could hardly wait. It was my sister's sixteenth birthday.

As dinner time approached, I was asked to shut the dining and living room drapes. I remember trying to figure out why we needed to close the drapes so soon, as it was only 5:00pm and barely dark outside. Mom replied that it was to keep the cool October air from sneaking in. Being only seven at the time, the answer satisfied my curiosity.

I gazed at the birthday presents, piled high at my sister's dinner place. The pretty bows, the boxes tied with curling yellow ribbon! Even the special birthday cake knife was decorated with a yellow bow and ribbon!

My dad had to add extra leaves to the dining room table to accommodate the extra places I had been told to set. I was

31

hoping and praying that there wouldn't be a kid's table tonight. I wanted to be in the middle of the action.

Backwards of our usual family birthday tradition, my sister got to open her presents first. She didn't have to agonizingly wait until after dinner and all the plates cleared to start the rip and tear. I hoped that when I got as old as my sister that this exception would be the rule!

There were "oooh's" and "aaah's" as she opened her gifts. I, quite frankly, was disappointed. I didn't understand why she was so excited to get clothes of all things. Where were the toys, the games, the fun stuff?

My sister's seat at the table was side center, her back to the sliding glass door. Earlier in the evening I had seen my dad slip out the door to sneeze and "honk his horn." *(That's what we called blowing his nose.)* On one of those times I thought I heard noises, but my dad said, "Oh, it must just be the breeze swirling around the leaves."

It was left at that. Little did we know when he slipped out it was to unlock the sliding glass door.

That's when suddenly several people barged through the unlocked sliding glass door. I thought we were being robbed. I screamed at the top of my lungs and quickly dove under the table. I knew under the table was a safe place. I had used it many times playing hide and seek after a big family event. And when the lace tablecloth was there, hanging to the floor, I was perfectly out of sight.

"SURPRISE!" The band of intruders yelled.

"No! You can't take her!" I said with a loud, piercing cry. I was so afraid of what was happening. Tears were streaming down my face. These people in disguise were dragging my sister—my protector, my supporter, my mentor, the person to whom I looked up to—away.

"Get away from my big sister, you big dummy!" I shrieked with my boldest of 7-year-old voice, kicking the shins of the person now grabbing my sister's legs.

These robbers were taking my big sister—and my parents were letting them! I was so confused. My dad's blue eyes were twinkling with glee as if he was glad to be rid of one of us kids. My mom was scurrying around, with a grin on her face no less, making sure her crystal and silver candle holders were not to be knocked over, unlike several of the dining room chairs.

"Let's haul her off!" I heard the ring leader bellow. "Her blind-fold is secure!"

The disguises were frightening to me, no question. I clung and held on to a table leg, sobbing and sobbing, fearing they might find me and take me next. I peeked through a hole and could see one person holding each leg and one person under her armpits. They struggled out the sliding glass door, and then they started to swing her.

"To sixteen!" the ring leader cried, "A one, a two, a three, a four! A five!"

"She's slipping!" I heard someone shout out, "Help!"

"A six, a seven, an eight."

Then . . . CRRRACK!

To this day I can hear the sound, clear as a bell, a shiver running up my spine.

The person who was holding my sister's head and arms slipped, my sister's head hitting the concrete patio floor . . . hard. Silence hung in the air, suspended in the moment.

My dad snapped into action, using his training as a volunteer

33

fireman. I heard crying and screaming, and watched as masks uncovered not robbers, but my sister's best friends. And there was no longer laughter.

All attention was focused on my birthday sister. I kept hidden under the table . . . afraid to move . . . afraid to speak . . . afraid to do anything else but stay hidden.

I have blocked much of what else happened that night, whether by fear or long-term memory loss that comes with my age. I vaguely remember the round-the-clock vigils her friends would have at the hospital and then at our home. I remember a variety of different baby-sitters who came so my parents could spend their evenings at the hospital.

It wasn't just some silly mistake—something an ice pack and Advil would heal. My beloved sister had suffered a severe concussion and back injuries. She was in the hospital for several days recovering.

I still remember sneaking into her bedroom while she was away at the hospital. I dug through one of her dresser drawers and took one of her pullover cashmere sweaters. I hid it in my pillow so I could 'feel' and 'smell' her close to me.

An evening of fun, excitement, planned with much love, turned into a night of terror for many. As I have reflected on the event over the years—and heard various accounts of it—I think of how one small incident, centered with love around one person, impacted so many people, in so many ways.

Different people reacted in different ways. Some brought food. Some baby-sat for free. Some just came and sat beside my sister in the hospital. Others kept at bay, their emotions and reactions too raw to realize it all came out well in the end.

Lessons of love and friendship are often hard. But love and

friendship, in its truest form, trumps fear, sadness and guilt. That is what my sister, all her friends and I found out that October. Time has healed most of the wounds and at class reunions the "Crack-up" story often comes up. It all ended with hugs, smiles, and even sometimes a few tears. But it ended. It was put behind us. And life continued on. That is, until 1970 when things really began to unravel. It would test the patience and fortitude of all of us. It would tear our family apart—quite literally—and leave us in pain for years.

The tenets of faith, family, friends and fun were about to be tested.

I had no idea how hard.

4

hold the fort

Approaching our city's lone stoplight, I braked carefully, making sure to come to a complete stop. I had long perfected the "jam and jolt" technique, but now it was time to show my parents I could prevent whiplash every time I stopped.

It was 1969 and I was fifteen years old. I was armed with a learner's permit and my parents' approval was high on my list of things to attain. I glanced to my right. I looked to my left. I checked my side and rear view mirrors, remembering the 3 second scan rule.

I wondered if my mother had worn a hole in the floor mat yet, as her foot always stomped the invisible brake each time she felt the need for extra help. Even though I was the third sibling she valiantly let drive her to and from high school, I knew she still was nervous. But there was something else on her mind that day—something that would change our family forever.

As we waited for the light to turn green, Mom casually turned to me and asked, "Care, do you think you can hold down the fort for a week or so?"

Quizzically, I asked, "Are you and Dad going somewhere special?"

I couldn't think of any school holidays coming up, so whatever was up had to be big.

"Well, I don't know if I would say *special* exactly," she said with a disconcerted sound in her voice. She sat quietly for a moment then continued. "I'm going to the hospital for surgery. I have cancer."

A long deafening pause filled the car. The air was sucked right out of my lungs.

I could not reply.

She continued the best she could, "Dad and I feel you are the best one to handle things while I'm gone. And, we don't want you to tell *anyone*—not your brother, not your sisters, not the teachers or staff at school! Dad or I will tell you when you can say something. Until that time, we are entrusting you with this *extremely* confidential and important matter."

The words out of her mouth dropped like a bombshell, shattering any resemblance of normal I had known up to that point.

"Why can't anyone else know? Why am I the *chosen* one? "Why *me*?" I asked.

Tears began to well up from deep within, clumping and chortling in my throat. Everyone knew, in those days the "C" word meant almost certain death.

"We need one of you kids to know," she replied. "It would be too hard for your brother with his college schedule right now. And, with your sister settling down back east, we don't want to worry her. Your younger sister, well, your dad and I think she is just too young right now. But don't worry. I'll be fine. You'll see. I'll be fine. I'll be back to your driving in no time!"

A faint smile was pasted on her lips.

The light turned green as silence hung heavy in the air. My mouth felt full of cotton. I tried to swallow, but the huge clump of choked back tears stayed dammed in my throat. A loud honk from behind startled me. Slowly, I eased on the gas pedal and rolled forward. For now, it was the only way I could go.

The days after the bombshell hit were hard. I wasn't sure I could keep quiet. I so badly wanted—so badly needed—to tell someone, yet I knew I had to be true to my word. It was my honor, and my love for my mother that kept my feelings bottled up. So, I continued, the best I could, with one foot in front of the other.

But my friends knew I needed something more if I were to make it through this storm. They could see it in my face. They knew I would need faith if I were to keep driving forward. That's when they introduced me to Club.

One of the "in" things to do on a Monday night growing up was Club (aka: Young Life Club). There were a number of reasons it was so popular. High on most people's list: they could get out of the house on a school night; it was a "church thing" so it must be safe; and it was full of really cute guys and all the popular kids.

I went mostly just to get out of the house. Sure, I knew it was a "God thing." That aspect of Young Life didn't bother me. I had been raised in a church (Episcopal/Catholic background). But as cancer made my mother sicker and as my dad let us kids know less and less, our responsibilities with household matters increased along with everyone's stress level. I looked for any excuse to get out of the house and with my friends. Young Life Club seemed like an easy solution.

I really liked Club. We had some wacky leaders like Brownie and Doug, Astrid, Jan and Jodie. They were all college kids who helped lead our time. There were fun skits like Chubby Bunny. And there were upbeat praise songs, not boring old hymns. Around Christmas, a favorite of Brownie and Silver was a rendition of "Chestnuts Roasting on an Open Fire." To this day—some 40 years later—it is still a Young Life hit . . . all around the world!

But there was one part to Club that got under my skin. It was the message. It wasn't preachy. It wasn't a sermon. It was real life talk. It was on my level, talking about real teen issues. . . and how God cared about me, right where I was, at that very moment.

They told me how God cared about me and how He wanted a relationship with me. Not just on Sunday morning or Saturday night confessional. Not just during communion, or on Ash Wednesday, Christmas, or Easter. God actually wanted to be my best friend. He wanted to come into my heart. He wanted me to know He cared. I just couldn't wrap my head around it.

There was too much going on at home. My whole life was in an upheaval. Everything that was supposed to be, wasn't. I was taken out of school part time to care for my mother as finances were tight and we couldn't afford private nursing. (Home health was just coming on the scene.)

I missed out on dating, on fun nights, on football and basketball games. College would be far-fetched, and I had to come to terms with my real reality . . . that my mother would die . . . hopefully soon. It was just too much for us all to handle.

On one particular Monday night, I came to the end of my rope. Or, should I say, I came to the end of myself. Week after week I had heard the message at Young Life about how God wanted to be a part of my life. But He was a gentleman and wouldn't barge in. I had to ask Him to come in. I had to ask Him to make, as the famous Christian booklet says, "My Heart, Christ's Home."

At this point, I was so very tired of my mom being sick. I was so tired of not getting to be a normal teen. I was tired of seeing my dad an emotional wreck.

I finally broke. An emotional basket case, I fled out of the room during the message. Two friends followed, worried that I might do something stupid. I assured them that I just had to clear my head and get this "Jesus thing" sorted out. We walked and we talked, and pretty soon, at their encouragement, even though I knew the "church thing" to say, they challenged me, "Tell God what you really think."

I wasn't sure He was ready to hear what I *really* thought, but I let Him have it! I told Him I thought death sucked. I told Him I thought I was getting a raw deal. I told Him, "Okay, this is it. I'm so tired of everything, and I can't go on."

I told God: "If you really want to be a part of my life, then take my mom to be with you. End her suffering. End her pain. You do that, and I'll believe you exist."

An uncanny peace came over me. No lightning bolt. No big boogey man. Just an incredible peace. And that was it.

Three days passed and nothing happened. I was beginning to wonder how this all would play out. Then, four days later, without a lot of warning, my mother died. I could hardly believe it.

No more walking on egg-shells. No more unfamiliar people walking in and out of our house. No more having to be taught how to change colostomy bags or bandages in my dad's absence when my mom, against every fiber of her being, would call softly for help. No more feeling like I should wear a sandwich board with medical updates instead of answering the multitude of caring, yet stinging questions like —"How's your mom today?"

No more driving my weakened mother to chemo or radiation. My parents had let me get my license on my birthday for that reason alone. There would be no more casseroles or calorie laden desserts or dinners in which to drown my sorrows. (I often found myself going for second helpings even when I'd lost my appetite. I should have just pasted the portions straight onto my thighs.)

I would lament the last semi-coherent words my mother would speak to me as I visited her for the last time. I was wearing my very first pair of Levi jeans. Her morphine-laced comment was, "Oh, sweetie, those jeans make your backside look like the broadside of a barn."

I didn't know how to respond—to her or my guy friend who had come with me. While I knew she wasn't used to the new look of tight pants, much less jeans on young women, the comment still stung . . . it still does.

Do I believe God caused my mother to die? No. She had terminal, stage four cancer. She was going to die. But did God use the situation to show me something? No doubt.

God showed me I had to humble myself. I had to be willing to come to the end of myself. I had to ask the hard questions. I had to believe, even if for me it meant throwing down a gauntlet of sorts.

That was more than 40 years ago and I have never looked back. I took God at His word. He has taken me at mine. Am I perfect? Far from it! But life is a process, with lots of trial and error. I'm still learning. I'm still often at odds with God. But I have a relationship with Him, not a religion. He is in my heart. And in my heart, He is at home. I don't know how I would have done life without Him—especially with the trials that were to come.

5

footprints in the sands of time

Through the years, God has brought some pretty amazing people into my life to encourage me at just the right time. Woody and Mackie were just those people. They were friends of my parents—dating back as far as middle school. And later in life, they would become my spiritual parents.

Woody and Mackie took me under their wings after my mom died. They shared life with me, as well as many truths and facets about being a Christian. The ideas were foreign to me. For, until that night at Young Life some nine months earlier, I had a "church" or "denominational" knowledge of God, Mackie and Woody and their three kids knew about the "relationship" part.

I will never forget that first Thanksgiving vacation after my mom died, driving down to Portland with the Woodward clan. We spent hours talking about the Four Spiritual Laws. For all I knew, the laws were a sub-set of the 10 Commandments. I had the hardest time grasping the concept. But by the end of that visit at a tender age of 17, I got what they meant. It was foundational in my life . . . and transformational.

Over the years I have stayed close to the Woodwards. We

have shared life, shed tears, and laughed until it hurt. And it wasn't just conversations about religion that kept us engaged and entertained.

I still remember, clear as a bell, a visit I had with Mackie just a few years back. It was a rare trip of mine through Portland, Oregon, and I decided to stay with her for a few days. My mother's close chum (as they referred to themselves), was now in her eighties. We had a delightful time, chatting up old stories, reminiscing, and selectively not mentioning others.

She told me stories of my folks, now long deceased, along with her spouse, many of which I had never heard, and some of which I would have rather not heard. Especially when it came to my parent's courting days.

"Did you know that I got my first *real* kiss from your dad?" Mackie mentioned somewhat half-heartedly.

I just about spit the pink lemonade across the room. That was too much information . . . especially from an 80-something, classy, up-scale woman!

She went on to explain how she and my mother, as eighth-graders used to go and check out my dad, Bob, and his friend, at the beach. They would hide behind trees and giggle, hoping not to be seen. They would wait for Bob—tall and lanky with drop-dead blue eyes—to dive off the dock. Then they would swoon.

I wanted my visual word pictures to stop!

My mother was so jealous, wanting badly for my dad to notice her. But no. He had his eye on Mackie.

Then one day, as the girls made their way to the bath house at Madison Park, Mackie lingered. She was hoping Bob would catch her. He did. And with that, he gave her a quick (but long enough) kiss on the lips.

What does one say to that?

To my relief, more stories followed. Stories that detailed how, in a true friendship manner, Mackie told Bob that my mom was the one interested, and that the other fellow was the one who intrigued her. The rest is history.

Today, I am still in contact with the Woodwards, now including Mackie and Woody's children and grandchildren—an ongoing reminder of what I call "Godcidences" (for there are no coincidences with God, only incidences He uses to impact our lives). Who else but God could plop the son and grandson of my mother's best friend in my life, some 60-plus years later, to see this heart story written and published?

Anne and Kent were a few of the other people that God brought into my life to make sure I stayed on the right path. They came into my life when I was in middle school, launching my lucrative babysitting career with their two incredible kids, Stu and Jenne. I can't tell you how many hours I spent listening to Stu's screeching attempts to eek out a violin piece. Months would pass and eventually I could make out the title of his earnest practicing.

When not screeching away, Stu would be enveloped with his passion for science, math, and on planes in outer space. Is it any surprise he is now a leading expert for NASA? Jenne would ever be the girl—first playing with dolls, then guinea pigs and dogs, and eventually her passion of soccer.

As months turned into years, her passion changed into homework and expert piano playing. Her compassionate and strong spirit carried her on to a bright career in psychology, and allowed her to courageously battle cancer. Oh how I loved those kids.

Being in Anne and Kent's home brought a sense of calm and belonging for me. I found refuge baking countless batches of cookies or scrubbing pots and pans for Anne during the tumultuous days of my mother's illness and death.

Anne had a sixth sense, somehow knowing exactly when I needed a time out and refuge from my daily life. She didn't even have to say anything. Her presence alone gave me a sense of acceptance, allowing my tears to trickle and my questions to be heard, all without judgment.

Anne showed me how to teach at an early age, bringing me under her wing as a pre-school Sunday school teacher. I honed my guitar playing skills on 3, 4 and 5 year olds. I sang "Jesus Loves Me" and "Deep and Wide" at least ten million times, and I can't count how many times I would collapse in laughter as we played Duck, Duck, Goose!

As I experienced the awkwardness of my teenage years and the immense struggle of watching my own mother die, Anne's gentle giant ways and listening ear were always there. The twinkle in her eyes, her silver fox hair glinting in the sun, she reflected the love that was greater than either of us.

Anne would not have been Anne if it weren't for Kent by her side. They were truly one and were the example for my future husband and me of what true marriage looked like. Their faith, their family, their hopes, and their dreams echoed in all they did. Relationships replaced things. Their effort was spent leaving their footprint in the sands of time—and they expected no less from me.

As they helped me through some of the most important times of life, their only admonishing was clear: "When you are in a position to give someone a start, take what we have given you, and give to someone else. Expect nothing in return."

Just a few months ago I received an email sharing the news of Anne's passing. It simply said: "Kent's dear girl and wife of 53 years has passed on to a better world."

Anne had lived with Alzheimer's disease for more than eight years. She had spent the last sixteen months of her life in assisted living. She had become too feeble to walk or feed herself. Hospice had been called in to help ease her pain until she crossed over to her better life. And I was heartbroken.

I'm sure you have received such an email or phone call. While the news may or may not have been expected, the wave of finality and grief washes over you. Maybe, like me, you let the tears stream down your face and allow yourself to succumb to heaving sobs. You knew the end was near, you knew that sweet relief had finally become a reality. That blessed peace had arrived. Even so, a hollow pit fills your stomach, and you weep.

You weep because you care. You weep because you love. You weep because you experienced something powerful, and now you're left to hold the fort.

Holding the fort can mean so many things. From holding strong to keeping confidences; Letting go and letting God, to learning that faith trumps fear every time.

The Godcidences of life are all around us—in our friends, in our mentors, in our parents, and in our everyday life. They are even in our generational family and friends, sent to keep our life compass set to what is true.

6

choose life

I wasn't sure what to expect as I put the key into the large solid oak door of my college dorm room.

How big would the room be?

Would I like my roommates?

Where would I sleep?

Was I the first to arrive?

Will I be able to sleep with two virtual strangers in my room?

What kind of music did they play?

The questions flew into my head like a swarm of bees returning to their hive.

As I turned the knob and pushed on the door, it creaked and moaned, slowly giving way to my new reality. There it was. The room lay stark naked except for three bare beds, three empty desks, and three small chests of drawers. This would be my home during my studies at the University of Puget Sound in Tacoma, Washington.

"So," I dismally said to my dad and step-mother, "this is it."

Since I was the first of the roommates to arrive, I took "squatter's rights"—the single bed, not the bunk! I could not even begin to conceptualize how three young women, total strangers, would fit their precious worldly possessions in this tiny basement dorm room. At least we had windows that opened to the ground above. A small consolation was that we were not far down the hallway from the community bathroom and showers.

Still uncomfortable with my father's new wife of less than a year, I longed to be alone with my dad to share one last "I'm still your little girl" moment before he left. Realizing that moment was not to be, I swallowed hard, snuffling down the crocodile tears that were welling up and threatening to spill over. I felt like a tiny sparrow being pushed out of the nest.

"I'd better get a move on!" I said, trying my best to mask my jumble of emotions. "I need to bring in the last of my stuff and finish staking my claim!"

What few possessions moved in with me were the only possessions I had to my name. My father's new wife had made it exceedingly clear to me as I was in my final packing mode that once I was out of the house, I was out. From that point on, only her things would be allowed in my old bedroom. While it was a hard pill to swallow, it was my new reality and my welcome to an adult world. From that day on, I never had a place I felt I could call home. That is, until I got married.

My step-mother's acerbic air made me want to make the impending goodbye short and sweet. I hesitated, knowing it meant cutting ties and closing an emotional door that would change how my father and I interacted, as long as she was in the picture. I knew things would never be the same, no matter how much I prayed . . . no matter how hard I tried.

I sat on the striped, bare mattress, wishing the moment away. In an instant, it would be over. My step-mother made an unconvincing attempt at letting me know how special I was in her life and how much she would miss me as she walked out the door. My stomach turned somersaults. I tried not to gag.

My dad held me tight, and with a twinkle in his eye said, "Remember to Matthew 6 it! I *know* you can do it! Remember that you're in Good Hands . . . and I don't mean Allstate!"

With that, he was gone. It was his way of letting me know that things would work out, even when two is company and three would be . . . well . . . interesting.

Oh . . . the early 1970s. What a time in history! Many compared it to aspects of the Civil Rights movement. But this? This was a movement all its own. Women's Lib was in full swing. Women joined the workforce in droves. Child-care outside the home became a viable option. And a favorite of many—the Burn the Bra Campaign—made the regular rounds on the nightly news.

One platform heard loud and clear on the college campus I attended was women's health. We had to attend mandatory seminars on date-rape and how to stand up for yourself. The importance of cancer prevention and education were out of the closet, into the news, and even on billboards. Women were encouraged to take responsibility for their health—medically, emotionally and for their social well-being.

Over the years, I've come to know that most women, no matter their age, tend to drag their feet when making an appointment for the infamous yearly exam. I don't blame them. Most people don't line up to have your body parts compressed and tightened, held in vice grips until your eyes pop out of their sockets and all semblance of air is squeezed from your lungs. I don't blame them for running the other way as the technician cheerfully chirps, "Are you sure I can't get this a little tighter?"

And that's not to mention the joys of freezer cold clamps, cotton swabs, and who knows what else!

For those who finally face the music and deal with the blissful exam, you are sent away with a cheery, "Look for your results in the mail or we'll call you!"

Each day, you run to the mail, check each phone call, and wait for the news.

I was no woman's libber. I was as naïve as they came. But I did get the message. I couldn't ignore the words, "Choose Life!"

Several weeks after the mandatory dorm meeting, I finally dredged up enough courage. That's when I picked up the phone and made "the appointment."

"TWO WEEKS?" I shrieked to the receptionist on the other end of the line. "I have to wait *two weeks* for the next appointment?"

Luckily, she only chuckled with understanding. Apparently the billboard advertisements were working overtime.

To my dismay, when I arrived at the office, my regular doctor was called out. His associate would be seeing me instead.

After the dreaded exam, I was surprised to be called back into his office. I knew it wasn't good. (I don't care whose office it is—the principal's, the boss', or the doctor's office—when you are called to the office, you *know* it can't be good.

As I sat down in the chair across from him, I was struck with fear. What was going on?

"To start with," the doctor told me, "I'm writing you a

prescription for the pill."

"What is *that* for?" I asked. It was clearly unsolicited.

"Well, you are in college, aren't you?"

"Yes," I answered.

"Well then, you most certainly will need these," he said.

"No, I won't," I countered.

"Yes, you will," he insisted.

"No, I won't. I'm *not* one of those girls. End of discussion."

He clearly didn't get it and went on to lecture me of all the pros and cons. I tuned him out until he finally changed the subject. But the new subject was no better. In fact, it was much worse. As I caught his words, my heart began to sink. Did I really understand what he was saying?

My lower lip started to quiver. Hot, stinging tears brimmed on my lower eye-lids.

"While we will have to wait for the results of the test to give us an official answer," he told me, "I am ninety percent sure that you have the beginnings of malignant cervical cancer."

My mind exploded with thoughts. *The C word? Are you serious? I'm only nineteen! My mother just died of cancer less than three years ago. This can't be happening. Not to me!*

"Did your parents ever tell you that your mother took the drug DES when she was pregnant with you?" he asked.

I looked at him with a blank stare. *DES? What was that?*

Talk to my parents? Right. Like I could, or even would, talk to my dad about female problems. And Mom? Well, we had just barely begun the woman-to-woman chats shortly before she died.

"No, they only told me that I was a preemie, born seven weeks early. I weighed only three and a half pounds," I snuffled.

55

Who could I tell? Where can I go? What do I do?

As if he could read my mind, the doctor responded, "Do you want to call your dad? Is there someone else who can be with you? I know this is hard for you, and will become harder. You see, you are the first generation of children born to a mother who took DES. It was a drug used in the 1940s and 1950s to prevent miscarriages."

My mind was still spinning.

"We don't know all the outcomes yet," he continued. "But, we are seeing a high number of cases of infertility for both males and females. We're also seeing female cancers of the cervix, ovaries, and uterus, as well as immune system deficiencies. Estrogen levels are typically low. That is the real reason I wanted to encourage you to be on the pill. I'm sorry I had to be the messenger. I was hoping your regular doctor would be here to tell you this."

I sat there silently, letting it process in my head as the doctor continued, "To be on the safe side—just to be sure—we would like to do a hysterosalpingogram. "

"A hippo-ping-pong-gram? Is that like a singing telegram?" I said, trying to lighten the air in the room.

"Let's make a deal," I continued. "I don't like door number one (this appointment). I certainly don't like door number two (the exam). So before I decide to walk through door number three (the hysterosalpingogram), I have to get outta here. I'll call you next week."

Door number three. Just what really could be behind it? Did I really want to know? I left the doctor's office and walked out in a numbing fog. I didn't know if I should go left, right, or stay straight on the steady course ahead? Could I trade doors?

Could I make a deal? And if not, then what?

I vaguely remember the 40 mile drive back to my college dorm. Hoping that I could play a poker face with my roommates, or at least avoid them for awhile, I went in my bedroom and shut my door. I flopped down on my bed, face first on the pillow, and began to sob. The tears that had been pent up for the last four years finally let loose. I pounded my fist in anger. I shouted from the depths of my soul.

I cried until I had no more to cry. Exhausted, I fell asleep.

Several hours later I awoke. Surely all that had gone on was just a dream, right? Isn't that what we all ask when something happens in our lives that we just can't believe?

I sat up and rubbed my eyes of the salty tears dried on my cheek. Knowing full well it was no dream, I made up my mind. There would be only one way to go into this next season. No whining. No excuses. Head on and head high. I would fight. And not only would I fight, I made a determination I would go forward with sincerity and authenticity. I would do this my way—being who I was—goofy, crazy Care.

First step was to do a little research. I still felt so in the dark. What was DES? Did my mom really take it? I needed answers.

Where, oh, where was the Internet back then? No WebMD. No Google. No Ask Jeeves. All I had was good old hard book research. It took time, but I found what I needed.

As I came to learn, in the late 1940s and early 1950s doctors and researchers were working hard to find a solution to help women who were unable to have children or who had a high rate of miscarriages. The drug diethystilbesteral—DES for short—seemed to be the answer.

For many, DES was the miracle drug that resulted in tiny bundles of joy. My parents were two of those people who were grateful for the drug. Having suffered several miscarriages, their physician felt that my mother would be a great candidate for the drug. But, they quickly found out, it came with a price.

One of the unanticipated challenges with the drug was that many of the pregnancies resulted in early deliveries, many ranging four to eight weeks early. I was no different. My due date was around the end of October. I was born the first week in September. And my weight? A slight three and a half pounds. My family would joke that I've always been in a hurry, never wanting to waste a minute of life, but really it was the DES.

In the 1950s, the neo-natal areas of the hospital were far from the high tech areas we have today. Back then, there were incubators where the tiny bundles would reside, under warming lights until their body weight and under-developed organs were able to handle life outside the hard, plastic box. Unlike today, parents were hardly able, if at all, to touch or hug or cuddle their pre-mature born child. That was my home for nearly a month.

Over the years I have followed the studies and research of DES offspring. It seems the males were only hit with pre-mature births and few suffered problems with infertility. The women, unfortunately, were not so lucky.

As time went on, we first-generation, female offspring came to find out the real side effects. It was found that there was an alarming rate of infertility for us. There was a high incidence of cervical and ovarian cancer. There was also a high incidence of thyroid and auto-immune deficiencies.

choose life

As I poured over the research and learned more about DES, I knew I would have to come to terms with this new reality. I had cervical cancer. I probably would have other issues . . . maybe more cancer. This was just the beginning. My life would be impacted by the choices my parents had made.

My head spun with all the facts, figures, and statistical medical research jargon. Did anyone *really* know what the outcomes would be? I hardly thought so. Soon I was bombarded by the physician's office with literature and offers to be in studies. Then vulture lawyers wanted to know if I wanted to join a class action lawsuit.

Suing, to me, would be to blame my parents and the doctors for doing something wrong. Giving me a chance at life was not wrong. Instead, they had given me a gift. Life was a gift. Sure, there was the unknown of the future. And the possibility of financial gain toyed with my carnal core. But who knew? Maybe my future would be fine. Maybe I would get through this little bout with cancer and be on my merry way.

I could hear my dad's voice echo in my ear (or was it God's?): "Remember Matthew 6 . . . you're in Good Hands."

With that, I shut the books. I shut the doors to the vulture lawyers. I turned down the studies. I wasn't going to give in to the fear of the future. I renewed my resolve to go forward with authenticity and sincerity. I wouldn't blame my parents for deciding to take the new drug. If they had known the impact it would have, do I think they would have gone for it? No way! I just wish mom was alive so I could let her know that I didn't blame her.

My parents chose life . . . for me.

For that I am eternally grateful.

7

living in the new normal

After choosing door number three, reality hit me hard. I knew I could never return to normal, nor was I really expecting to.

I wasn't surprised when the tests came back positive for early stage cervical cancer. After all the research on DES, it seemed somewhat inevitable. I would undergo several procedures, including more biopsies. Surgery to remove my cervix would follow.

Due to my age, and being a young college woman, they tried to preserve as much of my female anatomy as possible for future fertility possibilities. My days were a virtual physical and emotional roller coaster. Some days were good. Other days were excruciatingly painful.

With my mother's death, I was already tired of hospitals, doctors; now the hassle of commuting the 50 miles each way for follow-up appointments. But it had to be done. I would have to endure a special cryo-surgical procedure and repeat pap smear tests every six months. I screamed in silence each time the instruments poked and prodded at my decency—screaming more at the injustice than the torturous procedure.

I trusted my doctor. He had been my mother's physician. I didn't ask questions. I just went with the frustrating flow, and held it all inside. It was too painful to put into words.

Tears often came easily, and my heart ached more than words could express. Yet in a funny way, there were times hope stirred deep within. I just wished I had someone to talk to who could really understand.

Talking to dad was too painful. Plus, he's a guy. I didn't know how to broach the delicate subject. Besides, he was starting out on a new chapter of his life. My older sister was still in the process of moving from the East Coast to Tacoma and I didn't want to bother her until she got home. My brother and sister were both in colleges elsewhere in the state. We were all healing from mom's recent death. I didn't want to throw a damper on the lives of those I loved. But mostly, my own fears kept me from talking.

While I considered myself a social wallflower *before* receiving the devastating news about the DES exposure and its possible future ramifications on my life, I felt even more so now. But luckily, I now had a new living situation—a new support system that made it somewhat easier.

My college advisor, aware of some of what I was going through, heard that the university was looking for the first ever student "live-in" at the president's house; someone to nanny the three daughters of Dr. and Mrs. Phil Phibbs as well as help at social events. In exchange, I would have my own basement apartment with separate entry. My name was submitted, unbeknownst to me, so when Mrs. Phibbs called to offer me the position, I was caught a bit off guard.

As I learned what it entailed, I jumped at the chance. It was a responsibility I took very seriously. Nevertheless, I received much more than I gave. Little did they know the refuge and life line that they were extending.

While living at the president's residence gave me a place of isolation, I also found a place I could belong, albeit being an academic misfit and cultural geek. Their eldest daughter's life especially affected mine.

As I quizzed Kathy for her history tests, her infectious laughter exposed me to depths within myself. Kathy had courage to do things others shook their heads at (like becoming a chimney sweep after school). It would fuel my own desire to make a mark on my world, no matter what my family or friends thought.

Her sharing of their family travels, trials, and travails taught me how to listen better—especially to the still small voice in my heart; the heart of the I AM. It allowed me to step out, knowing what I believed and to "go up to the mountains and be a bearer of good news." Her dreaming helped me to dare to dream; to step out to live in adventure; to become, as my dear friends Dan and Judy say, "a dream maker for others."

Even now, years after a tragic ice climbing accident that took Kathy's life in 1991, her memory spurs me to climb even higher heights.

Kathy's mom, Gwen, filled an aching void I had felt since my mother's death three years prior. And Kathy's dad, Phil, made me feel like I had standing in an environment where I felt I had none. Kathy's much younger siblings, Jennifer and Diana, made me feel like I was the big sister again, at a time I sorely missed being around my own siblings.

But above all, Kathy reminded me that I had a friend, even

though I was housed in a basement—a campus away from my peers.

So while my friends were out partying, socializing and having fun, I turned my energy and focus to academics and life at the president's house. And I thank the Lord for it.

I thought I was headed towards becoming a teacher or getting involved with journalism of some sort. But Winterim— the January term that encourages students to explore avenues outside of their major—opened my eyes to a completely new field of interest. The redirection would change my life forever.

I sat on my bed, flipping through the course brochures for January Winterim. My first Winterim I had taken an introduction course to occupational therapy per the advice of my roommate and of "Coach"—the dean of women and my older sister's mother-in-law.

They both knew I was struggling, trying to make sense of my life after my mother's death. They could see that I didn't want just a career, but I wanted to leave my footprint and make a difference somewhere.

"Maybe writing or teaching isn't where you are meant to be," they had said.

I took the Winterim course "Intro to Occupational Therapy" and immediately felt at home. I had experienced first-hand the importance of a person retaining their health and independence, adapting as necessary, when I watched my mom walk out her final days. The idea of helping others do the same got me excited. I was good with people and enjoyed finding ways for them to function in their "new normal."

But I still wasn't sure that I could hack the rigorous pre-med science pre-requisites. I would have to shake my feeling of academic ineptness and pass anatomy and physiology and neuro-kinesiology before I could even think of declaring O.T. as a major. Living at the president's house was a perfect place to focus and study, but now it was time to find my second Winterim class to take.

I was ever so close to applying to the School of O.T. (there were only 15 slots available each year). I needed my "Matthew 6" resolve. My friend Kathy urged me to leap out of my comfort zone and do what I needed to figure it out. I decided if she could do it, so could I.

I approached the O.T. faculty and asked permission to do an unconventional Winterim. I wanted to use Winterim as a time for me to stretch, to finally deal with my mother's death, and take every ounce of adversity and every obstacle it had created for me and turn it into an opportunity and adventure. I would take my two week Christmas break to travel to Dexter, Maine to visit, share, and gain insight with my mother's brother, my Uncle Gordon.

Once there, I would research Elisabeth Kubler-Ross' new book *On Death and Dying*. I would write a three part thesis: the first on the stages of dying (or loss), the second based on my limited exploration of the O.T. field, and lastly, my experience with death—opening up and pouring my heart out about what I had walked through the past four years. My proposal, *Silence Like a Cancer Grows* was not only accepted, it awarded me one of the coveted positions in the School of Occupational Therapy when I applied that spring.

Little did I know how my late night study groups, my theological discussions with classmates, and Sunday evening Bible study groups would be additional preparation for the years ahead. The hours I spent working at social events, meeting people from around the world, and getting to know international figures who were guests of the president would open my eyes to things much bigger than I had ever imagined.

Sure, I may have been a social wall-flower, but it didn't mean I wasn't being exposed socially. All of these things would factor into my getting an internship at the Mayo Clinic and preparing me for the years when I would work in schools, home health, nursing homes, and even businesses with work-place wellness.

I had the joy of helping people with their physical, environmental, psychosocial, mental, spiritual, political and cultural factors that stood as possible barriers to their independent daily activities and occupation. I loved walking into a challenge. I loved working with an individual, challenging them to look at their limitations in a new light, and showing them the true possibilities that came with their new "adapted" normal.

Even more, I loved realizing I wasn't an academic misfit. I just hadn't found my right-fit, and O.T. was it.

The university position at the president's house was only for one year. They wanted other students to have the same opportunity afforded me. So when I returned for my junior year, I lived off-campus with a high school friend of mine. It was only a few blocks from the School of O.T., which was perfect.

My life was filled with very little social life, long hours of studying, and somehow I was able to squeeze in three part-time jobs to pay for tuition. The year seemed to fly by.

As the fall semester of my junior year was coming to a close, I found myself counting the days to the respite of yet another Winterim. It would be a welcomed break from the rigorous pre-med work. I was also looking forward to the visit from a few friends from Minnesota—the Minnesota J's as I would come to call them. They were coming to join me for an exchange term, and they were looking forward to a care-free month of fun and freedom.

The Three J's were quick to sign up for the Sports Appreciation course. They wanted something easy—something fun. Me? I was taking the "stretch" approach literally. I signed up for a philosophy course, thinking I would learn to think outside the box and be able to hold my own in a conversation with my Holy Names cousin who was getting her doctorate in philosophy. It didn't take long for me to realize I was in over my head.

My first hunch that the philosophy class was going to be a far stretch for me was the sheer weight of the books that I would have to read in one month's short time. The second—I could barely pronounce most of the philosopher's names. I was dead meat and I knew it.

I stumbled out of the class on that first day, bleary eyed and swaying from the weight of the books. I could barely think about the four hundred pages we had to read by the next afternoon. As I got to my bedroom, the whining started. *What did I do to myself? How on earth could I have even thought I could handle this? Why didn't I opt for the pass/fail route? Instead, I*

*elected to have the grade boost (or bomb) the all-important GPA.
What was I thinking?*

A knock on my door interrupted my pity party. It was the
three Minnesota J's. They were talking over each other as they
came barging into the room. Each one was louder than the
other, crooning on about what a great class they had, how much
fun it was going to be, what a cinch it was, and . . . how many
great guys there were. Then, as if in unison, they all stopped and
looked at me. I was pale as a ghost, a slight green tinge coming
over my face.

"To Engine House No. 9!" one called out.

That was all it took. We were off.

Engine House No. 9 was a favorite watering hole for kids on
campus. Just a few blocks from campus, the red brick fire house,
built in 1907, had been turned into a fun little pub and had
gained the reputation as one of the area's premier hang outs. At
the time, I didn't really care. I just needed to get out.

Over a pint of diet soda (I wasn't yet 21) and their pitchers
of beer, I lamented over what I had done. I could no more
return to that class and hold my brains together than I could fly
to the moon. What was I going to do?

The three J's answer was simple: transfer into their class! And
the arguments were rather convincing. The male/female ratio
was incredible. (They were the only girls in the class.) The grade
would be a cinch. And, best of all, we would all be together for
the entire month.

My mind raced. Could I actually do it? Did I really have the
guts to drop a class and join my friends as they hung out with
30 college men for the entire Winterim? My friends stayed on
me throughout the night. They wanted me in the class. They

wanted me with them, experiencing a new reality.

I wasn't sure if I could bring myself to do it. I thought back to those silly games we played as kids. Spin the Bottle. Double Truth or Dare. This was more frightening to me than any of those. And then there were the guys.

During my mom's illness, I had become a stress eater. Within the last year I had finally lost the excess 50 pounds. My "insulation" and reason not to date was no longer there to protect me. I couldn't believe I was even thinking this way!

The three J's kept prodding through the night. While they were getting tipsy, I was getting cold feet. I had never had a "steady" date. I had never had a "real" kiss. The two sides of my conscience kept banging my brain, each pleading their case. Even to my surprise, the radical side seemed to be winning the argument. But I had one requirement—that we would never enter class alone. One for all, and all for one.

We were well into the new Winterim class and I had yet to enter class alone. So far, we had all held up our end of the bargain, and I had actually found myself enjoying the new reality. (The attention from the guys in the class no doubt was helping.) Things had been good—an exciting adventure. Until now.

7:58 . . .

7:59 . . .

7:59 and a half . . .

8:00 . . .

Do I dare risk the 10 point deduction every minute I am late? I thought to myself. *Where are those girls?*

The rule was clear. One for all, and all for one. The J's had never been late.

8:01 . . .

8:02 . . .

8:03 . . .

That's it. Here goes nothing.

There is nothing like walking the full length of a field house basketball court, every step echoing through the cavernous auditorium.

Squeak, squeak, clomp, squeak.

I was already blushing. I scanned the class, assembled in the bleachers. Up one row. Down the other. Back and forth. No . . . I must have missed them. Look again. Maybe the teacher, an infamous practical joker, was hiding them somewhere.

Suddenly, the class broke out in song. It was a chorus from the *The Hills Are Alive* from the *Sound of Music*. Each step felt like I had 100 pounds of lead in them. The men stood up, gave me a standing ovation.

The instigator of this whole little ploy, one of the most shy men in the bunch (in spite of his 6 foot frame, 22 inch neck, and 52 inch chest) finally came forward and said: "We have thought these last few weeks that it just isn't right for you to not have a "J" name. So, today, we are dubbing you Julie, like in Andrews. You look and act so much like her, and your roommate tells us you sing like her too!"

It was Mr. Bill. He and his company were the culprits of the outburst. And I can't say I was all too upset. Sure I was embarrassed. But I had been gazing at Bill from a distance ever since I joined the class. I loved his deep brown eyes and his massive frame. I had even caught him looking at me and blushing himself, embarrassed that I'd seen him sneak a peek.

Earlier in the week I had seen Bill in action as the Ninth-in-the-Nation heavy weight wrestler at a home match. He bear-hugged a 350 pound behemoth of a man and, as he had him suspended in the air, I heard a voice yell out: "So now what are you going to do with him, clown?" (It turned out to be his dad!)

I don't think Bill had thought that far in advance, but he gently lowered the massive teddy bear and pinned him. I could only imagine how someone so strong could be so tender as well. As I left the match I heard some of the cheerleaders say to one another: "Did you see that big guy? I wonder what they feed him?"

Then a voice from a woman standing all of 5-foot-nothing said: "Raw meat, every meal! I'm his mom, I should know!"

I smiled as I went my way.

Little did I know that my current college roommate, Terry, and another good friend had plans to introduce me to Bill already in the works. I had been battling the infamous Hong Kong flu and dragged myself to more than half the classes that January. I had missed the sessions on wrestling, and that exam was coming up. Terry knew I really needed Bill's help, and set up a house study date.

The "date" was benign. Truly just a study date. I imagined that he, a big fraternity guy and popular athlete on campus, could have any woman he wanted. I knew women he dated had long hair, were well-endowed, and were very feminine. Me? Just think of Julie Andrews or Jamie Lee Curtis. Girlie-girl? Well, *True Lies* did have its moments!

Bill was handsome, smart, amazing, tender, and he had a

voice that could send chills down your spine when he sang.

Study date over, I was back to my wall-flower self. Oh, I would dream of a date with Bill, but who was I kidding? I would never be in the running. I would never even be close! Come to find out, he was keeping his distance as he was nursing his wounds from a hard break-up. I had not been aware of the relationship. It was all Greek to me, literally.

While Bill and his friends ran in the fraternity circles, I was an "independent" from the "other side of the tracks/campus." Bill and his ex had made a pact that if they were still "in love'" when she returned from a semester abroad, they would talk about getting married. She returned. Feelings were gone. And he was crushed.

The bigger they are, the harder they fall.

All his friends knew how hard Bill was taking it, especially his ex, my childhood friend, Rin. But she really wanted Bill to be at her wedding. And yet, she knew he would never come unless there was a good reason.

Enter Care.

I had just undergone another knee surgery. The ravages and ongoing struggle with degenerative joint disease from being exposed to DES was in full swing. I was in a hip to ankle cast. I was scheduled to be in Rin's wedding, but of course, I could not drive. According to Rin, that would be the perfect reason to get Bill to the wedding. She would ask him if he would bring me and make sure I got home okay. The rest is history. Or should I say a *Godcidence*?

After Rin and Ray's wedding, Bill and I went out to dinner and talked for hours. He told me about growing up on a dairy farm at the base of Mt. Rainier, in Enumclaw. (Ironically, it was the place my dad dreamed about moving to once he retired.) He shared about his three sisters and their many antics growing up. He told about his family, full of love and laughter. He shared the hurt of losing his sister in a terrible motorcycle accident. She was just three years older than Bill.

We cried together, sharing our hearts about the ones we loved and lost and how hard it was to let them go. I shared that I dreamed of getting pregnant one day, but DES may get in the way. We talked about God and the place He had in his life.

We drove for several more hours in his 1967 MGB, the top down, the moon and stars twinkling overhead. Bill said that since the study and wedding dates were set-ups, they didn't count. That's when he asked me out on a *real* date.

Today, *Blazing Saddles* and the campfire scene are forever written on our hearts. Bill "knew it" then. And me? Well, it took me about two weeks. We waited for two months to announce our engagement. And today, 35 years later, we couldn't be happier.

Our marriage grows stronger each year, his proposal saying it all. That Sunday afternoon, in my campus house kitchen at 4:12 in the afternoon, kneeling on one knee, Bill placed a white sapphire ring (my birth stone) on my finger. The ring was a family heirloom, having originally been a stick pin for his great-great-grandfather, made into a ring for his great grandma, and passed down through the generations. This is what he said:

"Lady . . . will you marry me . . . be my wife . . . my lover . . . the mother of our children . . . but most of all, my best friend . . . with God's help?"

A year and two days later, we married and moved to his hometown at the base of those hills of Mt. Rainier.

I'm glad I took a chance that Winterim. I'm glad I risked enough to experience a new reality. And yes, the hills truly *are* alive . . . everywhere we have lived.

8

homesick, heartaches, and heroes

I don't think anyone is prepared for marriage. How can they be? You go from the sweet pitter-patter of the heart, to romance, to planning . . . then *poof*!

Bill and I had been caught in the whirlwind of all the plans. I was also working feverishly to finish my senior year of college. Before I knew it, finals were upon me and I jumped right into my in-patient psych internship. There's nothing like a fresh, off the docks shipment of the drug PCP (an animal tranquilizer, usually reserved for elephants) to hit the streets of Tacoma.

As a new grad, I trembled. I felt hardly prepared to treat these vulnerable, weary, worn, and profoundly addicted people. I was spent by the end of my first rotation, but there was no rest for the weary.

A week later, I was off to my physical disability/surgical internship at the Mayo Clinic in Rochester, Minnesota. We were penny poor, but rich in love and filled with faith. I had to venture out alone, without Bill, for those six months. It wouldn't be easy.

I had just unpacked my bags in the all women's nursing dorm when I got the phone call. It was my dad. His best friend from middle school, Woody, had died the night before. Standing in stunned silence, thousands of miles away from anyone who knew me, on my first day in a strange town, I couldn't believe my ears.

Woody had been a powerful example and mentor in my life. He had sown so much to ensure my faith was firmly rooted. And now he was gone.

My dad relayed the sad story to me over the phone. Woody was at a send-off dinner for internationally known evangelist Luis Palau. Woody had gone up to speak to the evangelist when he collapsed from a brain aneurysm in Luis's lap.

I wanted to run. I wanted to run home. I wanted to be at the service. My dad asked one simple question: "What would Woody want you to do – come and cry, and be sad? Or, stay, cry, and be sad . . . but reach out to others as he did, sharing Matthew 6?"

I knew I must stay.

The six months away from family were brutal. Thankfully, I had an occasional weekend respite away in the Twin Cities, visiting one of my favorite high school teachers. She had become my mentor, just as my mom had been hers. Allie's first year of teaching was my mom's last year of life. Allie and I have stayed close. We have shared many journeys together, including cancer—each personally and with family members. We got involved with Relay for Life® as team captains and committee members.

Even with the weekends away, the rigors of internships

caught up with me. The total weariness was caught on camera by the Minneapolis Star for their Christmas Eve edition. There I was, in a horrendously long line, at the Minneapolis-St. Paul airport.

I was sitting on my carry-on baggage, my eyes were glazed and head was downcast. My chin was resting on my balled up fist, elbow on my knee. The caption read: *Coming . . . going and . . . waiting.* Weather related flight cancellations were about to ruin any thought of spending my first married Christmas in the arms of my beloved. Tears threatened to break out at any moment.

Providentially, a window of opportunity opened and our flight got out. Before I knew it, I had returned to be enveloped in that all comforting, protective hug of my husband, and that's when we officially started our married life together.

The months flew by as I started my job as a full-fledged, registered, licensed occupational therapist. I worked at the local hospital and school district, as well as the local pool, teaching adapted aquatics and coaching the swim team.

Working in the schools, I loved it when a class would have P.E. at the local swimming pool. It was so much fun doing adapted therapeutic activities and exercises in the pool with the kids with whom I worked. It never ceased to amaze me how much freedom they finally had once they were in the water.

Weightless and without their cumbersome braces—their twisted, frail limbs could move like those of their peers'. Their excited chatter and delightful laughter was contagious. Pool time was the highlight of their week! For once, they were normal—moving around just like their classmates.

Living in the small, rural community of Enumclaw where I

worked, running into people I knew was a common experience. And that included the kids with whom I worked. Admittedly, sometimes it was hard when people remembered me, and I didn't recall them. *Were they once a patient of mine or a family member?* I would wrack my brain. *Were they a classmate or a volunteer? Did I see them at the hospital, the school, the pool? Could I ever remember their name?*

Never did I think that I would be the center of the confusion until one day, a child who I had worked with at the pool came racing up to me in her wheelchair at the grocery store. Nor would I know how much explaining I would quickly have to do as I stood at the checkout line.

"Teacher, teacher!" she loudly squealed. "You look so funny with your clothes on!"

Oh . . . out of the mouths of babes.

I relished being married and racing ahead at a frenzied daily pace. I was a city girl turning country, just like Kate and I had dreamed so many years ago. I was getting used to the town's aroma of freshly spread cow manure, raising chickens, turkeys, and even learned how to castrate our bull calf! I never knew *that* was in the "I do!"

It was a settling time of getting to truly know each other's bents and habits. Bill and I laughed often. We enjoyed making new friends over fondue and entertaining old friends whose stories gave me new insight to the man I thought I really knew. But the most I learned about my husband came from Darrel, the best man in our wedding.

Darrel's heartfelt remarks came in an email several years after marriage. He had written a piece about my husband for a local publication, and he felt the need to share it with me. We both were struggling through our own difficulties, and he knew the article would lift my spirits. It speaks for itself.

I want to share it with you, my reader, so that you know the person who is the wind beneath my wings, who loves me and cherishes me like no other, and who helps me cope no matter what befalls us:

I think of him every time I travel to Kent, a nearby town, to visit with my wife at work. I go out of my way to travel down the old country road past his childhood home. It's still there, as are the memories. When we were in high school he and his family moved into town and I passed that house daily on the way to school. The memories are still there too. I rub my shoulder and I swear that I am still sore from the bruise he gave me out on the playfield at Bryon Kibler Elementary when we were both in the first grade. I remember when he took me off the wrestling mat in a fireman's carry because I fell into a hypoglycemic shock. And I remember the hug we shared just before he left with his new bride and my new friend.

I grew up with him. We competed in sports against each other and with each other. We sang in choir together and chased the same girls. I was the better looking guy but he got the better looking girls. We were both the sons of hard working men and rarely would we ever cross the boundaries they set. We were good, respectful sons, but we got into our share of trouble too.

When my children were small they would always ask for another "Crazy Bill" story. I would tell them over and over and I'm sure the embellishments I added still hold some of the truth intact. Admittedly, I would always tell my children that it was "Crazy Bill's "idea that would get us into trouble.

My sons respect him, my daughter idolizes him, and still I don't know how to describe him. But in truth, he probably cares little about definitions, except maybe that he be known as a son of God and a devoted husband and father.

Bill was the kid I looked up to when my world first closed in on me when I lost my hearing in the first grade. I gained some of it back but not before most kids nicknamed me "Huh." That was my usual response when they would say something I didn't understand. Imagine always being "it" or never knowing what football play was being run. Bill always looked directly at me and talked loud enough for me to hear. And he never called me "Huh."

Bill and I learned how to wrestle together and spent six years on the same team. When I came down with diabetes in my senior year of high school, he was there. More of the world closed down around me, but Bill stayed with me and let me live in the capacity that I could.

He listened to me when my first marriage disastrously fell apart and much later when I remarried. We shared stories of our children growing and I was there when his daughter was married. I was in the next room when his mother passed away and I was at his father's funeral.

But what was most important to me was that Bill would let me have fun. When others would "overprotect" me, Bill would encourage me to do things, to discover things much like when we were children. I got to go boating and snow machining with him. He would point things out to me as we drove. Through his beautiful eyes I was able to discover these things. I was a child again.

With my kidney disease closing down more of my world, I know that there is at least one place I can visit where I can have fun and still be able to get the dialysis that will dictate what I can do for the rest of my life. Bill will be able to look directly into my wife's eyes and assure her that I will be watched over, and my wife will believe him.

So how do I describe a guy who is so fundamental to my life, who has exceeded any description of friendship? Maybe hero is the proper word.

And so life went on. Friends, family, our faith intact, and yes, we were having fun as newlyweds. We worked hard. We played hard. We lived each day to the fullest—fast and furious. And I loved our frenzied pace.

So when I started to drag and had constant flu-like symptoms of fatigue and nausea, being young and newlyweds of sorts, we began to actually get excited. Maybe, just maybe, I was pregnant! Oh, our dream come true! Well, not exactly the best timing. But hey, just maybe . . .

Then the tragic words came: "We're so sorry."

The words hung heavy as a thick descending fog, the actual tone muffled in the post-anesthetic daze of semi-consciousness, not yet being able to discern dream from reality. The "flu" or hopeful pregnancy had turned into something more serious overnight.

It was cancer.

The muffled voice continued, "The cancer we found, plus the DES your mother took to prevent miscarrying you and ultimately giving you life, will keep you from bearing the children you so desperately want."

From deep within a sharp cry surged, unable to be released. Agony from the words, and a pain more excruciating than death itself, struck every fiber, every muscle, every nerve and cell of my body. All that we had longingly dreamed of, prayed for, saved for, diligently planned careers around, collapsed with those three small words.

The medical team that surrounded us were our friends—my co-workers from the small rural hospital where I worked. As word of our disappointing news made its way around our small intimate town, people sent their well-intentioned regards.

Yet each card, each phone call, each face to face encounter served only to remind me of the void I felt deep within. Somehow I felt that I had failed. I had failed my husband, failed my in-laws, and failed my own family. I had deprived them of a blood link to their past, and a hope for the future.

Living in a rural town, babies were a thriving part of the

hospital where I worked. My spirit would be pierced when I would walk through the nursery, another reminder of infertility stabbed relentlessly.

Other times, tears would well up as I longingly watched full-term mothers walk the hospital halls or a newborn held close to a young mother's breast. Where was the justice? It just didn't seem fair. We, who so desperately wanted to share the miracle of life, the gift of God, ironically and curtly denied because of a drug meant to save and bring me life.

After agonizing months, we settled into a routine, and realized that our dream didn't die. There were other options—other ways to see our dream fulfilled. That's when we decided to adopt. We weren't prepared for all the legal jargon, the myriad of reference letters, resumes, and recommendations. But it was worth it. As we made our way through the jungle maze process of adoption, we held on to hope!

Yet time and again, words such as "too young" or "history of cancer" or "a traditional stable home environment would not be provided as the husband would be job-sharing and assisting in the child care" kept us from our dream. But more often than not, it was the financial cost that would keep the door closed. We knew we couldn't muster the thousands of dollars it would take for an "instant" family.

Weary and financially drained, we could only rely on and rest in our convictions that if we truly *were* to have a family, somehow circumstances would need to change. Our strong faith in God would have to prevail and provide. Somehow, some way, we knew we could be strong. We had each other. We had family and friends. And we had faith that God was in control, even when we thought otherwise.

9

whose normal are you living?

Life resumed its daily routine until January of 1979. We received a call from the very physicians who had given us our childless sentence. To their amazement, we were told that there would be, for the first time in ten years, a baby available for private adoption. The baby would be ours if we wanted it.

So the question was simple: Did we want the baby?

Does the sun rise in the East? What kind of question what *that?* Of course we wanted the baby! There was just one catch. The doctors and nurses would have to convince the young seventeen-year-old mother not to give the baby to an agency... and even more ... they had to convince her that we were the right choice.

The mother was insisting that the baby go to a home where both parents were active, strong Christians. The only thing we knew to do was go to God in prayer and wait for His will to be done.

The days leading up to the birth were tension-filled. It was as if we were watching a tightly matched game of tennis. Unbeknownst to us, a close friend of ours was monitoring the pre-natal care and co-workers of mine would be delivering the baby. Could it all be done in the strictest of confidentiality? No names exchanged. Complete protection of information.

And even more, would I be willing and able to leave my job and not set foot in the workplace or the hospital as soon as the mother went into labor? In our hearts, we undeniably knew the answer.

As the days turned into weeks, my thoughts often settled on the mother. Here was a young seventeen-year-old girl, caught in what we were told was a forced pregnancy. She was just a mere girl, with hopes and dreams of a college education and a career on which she would set her sights. She was a young Christian woman with the maturity of someone twice her age—humbly setting the needs of her unborn child ahead of her own. She knew, in agony, that it would be best for the child and ultimately herself . . . even the father.

But could she really go through with it? Could she really give her child over to someone else? Would they love the child as she did? Would the adoptive parents know the pregnancy was full of love and tender care? Could she literally be severed from a part of herself, knowing she may never see the child again? Could she give the ultimate gift of life and thus renounce a sentence of doom? "Could she not . . ." she wrote in an anonymous letter to the unknown parents.

To our utter joy, she stood strong. And on May 25, 1979, Jamie Marie was born. We were told that she bore the very resemblance of her birth mother. As the days and months and years have slipped by, the memory of this courageous young woman and father has not. We continue to pray for them and thank God for them—truly a miracle in our lives.

Although we may never be lucky enough to thank them in

person, we hope by grace that they truly know that their little one is loved and loves in return. It is the same love she was given at birth—the very love God gives to us all.

Our son Tim would come into our lives five years later, in just as miraculous and inconceivable a way as Jamie, but with very different circumstances.

"Are you sure we are doing the right thing?" I asked Bill as we drove. "How will we know for sure? Do you think we are getting in over our heads? What if it all backfires?"

My questions pelted my husband faster than the windshield wipers could wipe the sleet-like snowflakes.

"Will you settle down?" he replied gruffly. "We have four more hours to drive until we get there. If you don't stop badgering me with your ridiculous questions, I'll stop the car right here, right now, and turn around and go home."

I sat glumly, watching the wipers swish back and forth. We drove in silence.

"Sweetie, where is your faith?" Bill softly said to me. "Try to sit back, relax! Enjoy the winter wonderland."

Hrumph!

I turned my back and flung my head against the car window. My stomach churned like stubborn cream being hand-whipped into butter. The miles crept by like days and the hours dragged by even slower.

It all had started with a phone call. One of those phone calls that wake you up on the one morning you planned to sleep in.

"Care?"

I didn't answer for a moment, trying to clear my cob-webbed morning head.

"This is Jean from the Department of Social and Health Services," the cheery voice on the other end of the line chirped. "I hope I didn't wake you, but I couldn't wait! I have great news for you!"

I sat silently, still trying to process the early morning call.

"You know," she replied. "Jean? Your case worker?"

My lack of response led her to believe I didn't know who was on the other end of the line. I did.

I quietly groaned, "Oh, hi, Jean. What's up?"

"You'll never believe it! You came up as a perfect match with a child for you to adopt! You were number one on all the computer questionnaires and paperwork from all the applicants in the state! I'm so excited! Aren't you?!"

I didn't know what to say. I sat dumbfounded. Yes, we had been on the adoption list for years. Yes, we had desperately desired another child and were praying to God for Him to provide. But circumstances in our lives had recently changed. As a result, we had requested to have our names removed from the adoption list weeks ago. In fact, just days earlier, our lawyer asked us if we were going to pursue adopting another child. The response was clear and concise. No. Another child was not in the offing.

Our plans had changed drastically over the past several months. Health issues and a serious car accident had left me a little more worse for wear. We were also feeling called to the mission field. We had shifted much of our attention to my recovery so we could head overseas. And the decision had been made that one child would be easier to handle on the mission

88

field, and financially it would be much more feasible.

I slowly ambled out of bed, and procrastinated through the day's routine of therapy exercise and chores. The phone conversation with Jean nagged at me, consuming my every thought. I prayed throughout the day, asking God for peace and direction.

"Maybe, just maybe, Bill would change his mind?" I mused. But yet, there was no mistaking Bill's emphatic "no" when he told our lawyer we were not going to adopt another child. And it wasn't often that you could change Bill's mind.

I couldn't stand it any longer. I jumped into the car and drove over to Jean's office. I knew Bill would blow his top if he knew what I was doing.

I met Jean at her office door and continued our conversation from earlier. I tried to explain there was no way we could take this child. Bill had said "no," and that was that. I had no reasonable explanation for why I was even there. And then I blurted it out.

"Could I peek at the picture . . . since I'm here?"

That's all it took. Something stirred deep within me as I laid eyes on the precious little boy. I knew I had to at least tell Bill. Never mind the details that he had mild cerebral palsy and autistic tendencies from being raised in a frightfully abusive situation. Never mind the fact that he looked so much like Jamie at that age. There was something else about him. I just had to tell Bill.

It was a task I feared was impossible. Bill was working 14 hour days drilling rock and a decision would have to be made by morning if we were going to pursue this adoption.

I practically accosted Bill when he arrived home. He gave me the answer I knew would be coming.

"What part of 'no' don't you understand, Care?" he said.

I let it go.

Several hours later Bill came to me.

"When do we have to let them know?"

I slowly turned my head back to Bill. One last time, as the snowflakes pelted the window, I barraged him with questions.

"How will we REALLY know, Bill? Is this even possible? Are we sure we want to do this?"

"Look . . . I already told you." He answered. "I will know the minute I look in his eyes."

By the time we pulled up to the foster home where Tim was living, I could barely contain myself. I was practically out of the car and on the doorstep before Bill even had a chance to turn off the engine.

I still remember the moment as if it were yesterday. Tim was playing quietly at a corner table, trying to piece a puzzle together. His hands moved erratically, the result of neurological impairments and delays from years of neglect and abuse. He chattered to himself, a jumble of vowels and consonants. His speech was significantly delayed. At five years old, he barely seemed three. We were told he was just learning how to walk without falling.

Tim had no idea who we were, or why we had come to visit.

As we entered the room, he gazed up at Bill. Tim's big chocolate eyes widened as he took in Bill's 6 foot, 210 pound frame. Bill, the former wrestler, bent down to meet Tim's gaze.

"Hey, Tim!" Bill said softly. "What's your favorite thing to do?"

"I wuv to wessel!" he squealed, throwing his arms around Bill in a bear hug and knocking him to the ground.

Misty eyed, the national heavyweight wrestler choked, "I know."

Raising kids on a good day is challenging enough. But raising kids in our family, with *my* medical challenges, brought even more challenges. Finances were tight. Days were long. And it seemed someone, mostly me, was always dealing with some sort of serious issue. It made our lives anything but normal.

My good friend DES would continue to show its ugly head as we tried our best to live our normal lives. The ravages of the drug would continue to hit me. There would be many frightful times in the kids' lives as they dealt with my fractured body. We took it in stride—the best we could. But some times were harder on the kids than others. I remember clearly one of the times when fear about DES related cancer hit Jamie's little heart.

I was going over my list for the umpteenth time to make sure the "new normal" would actually run as "normal" as possible after my thyroid cancer surgery. I was scheduled to go in to surgery the next morning, and we had just informed the kids that night. Jamie had been snuggled in bed for quite a while. Even so, I could hear her tossing as her box spring mattress squeaked. I sat down for a minute, gazing at the fire, with the flames dancing on the logs. I was trying to wrap my head around my surgeon's admonishment.

"We caught this tumor rather early, so things are in our favor. So, relax and trust me, and trust God. Neither of us has failed you yet, have we?"

I had to chuckle.

Pretty soon I heard a pitter patter of footsteps down the stairs. Jamie came down and stood before me. Big crocodile tears were forming on her lower eyelids. She kept snuffling to keep them from spilling over. Her little chin was quivering. I scooped her up and sat her in my lap.

"What's the matter, sweetie?" I said. "Is it too warm upstairs for you to sleep?"

"No . . . that's not it." She snuffled. "Can, can, can I comb your hair?" she stammered.

At first I didn't know quite what to say. I gulped down a chortle, trying to be ever so careful as to not make worse whatever serious matter was bothering her. (You must understand—for over 40 years I have had a Jamie Lee Curtis short hair cut—even I don't comb my hair. I just rumple it with hair gel each morning and go!)

"Why, sure! Go grab your brush!" I was finally able to say, without a chuckle sneaking out. As I sat on the couch, she methodically brushed and stroked my hair. I felt a drip hit the top of my head. Then I felt another. This one hit my nose.

I turned around and quizzically looked up at Jamie.

"Oh, Mommy," she choked. "I just don't want two bald parents!"

I reached around and hugged her. I held her tight and prayed with her. I showed her God's Words of promise to "take care of me always." (And that I wouldn't come home bald like her dad!)

Teachable moments of reassurance, faith, and love—along

with laughter and hugs. *These are the ways we will make it through, sweet Jamie.* These are the ways we will make it through. Through knee surgeries. Through breast cancer, and even more. This is how we would make it through . . . even house fires or volcanoes could not hold us back.

That's right. Volcanoes . . . in our back yard.

Did I mention life is an adventure?

It was May 18, 1980. We were on our way to church, just outside beautiful Cowlitz County. We took two cars that day as we were teen leaders and had a pool party. Bill's folks were driving from two hours away and would arrive before the party was over. They were coming to see our new home. The phones had just been hooked up the night before and we hadn't had a chance to let anyone know our number.

Just down the road from our house was a perfect spot to look at Mt. St. Helens. I signaled Bill, who was driving behind me, to stop. Mt. St. Helens was gorgeous – all adorned in snow, a small puff of seismic steam jetting out the top. The sun was shining brightly, its early morning rays on the northern slopes. We snapped a couple of post-card photos, as was our routine to chronicle the mountain's activities for our photo album. We kissed each other and were off.

Bill headed for the freeway, but I stopped for gas at the convenience store. As I was pumping gas, I saw first one, then two, then four, then six emergency vehicles pass. *Oh, Harry Truman and the Red Zone locals are probably stirring up a ruckus,* I thought.

93

"Anyone know what the commotion is?" I asked.

"Nope. Nothing here. Not even on the C.B. radio," the clerk replied.

The locals sitting at the breakfast bar shook their heads as well.

I headed back to my little orange VW Bug, towards the freeway and church.

When Bill and I finally made it to church, our friends flocked over to us.

"Did you hear?"

"Did you see it on your way down?"

"Is your house okay?"

"Do you have to evacuate?"

We were barraged with questions. I stared blankly back at them. I didn't have a clue what they were talking about. That's when I turned my head to look through the large church window. In horror I saw gigantic, black and gray plumes spewing higher and higher, heading upwards and then east.

Mt. St. Helens had blown!

As church radios blared from the back pew, Bill and I contemplated whether to stay or leave. We were paralyzed. Where on the road were Mom and Dad? Oh, I wish we knew where they were. They would know what to do. They would know what to say to us and how best to direct us.

We decided the best thing was to stay put. The freeways and roads we had just driven on were now closed and placed in the Red Zone. Our house of just one week was now possibly in harm's way. This was new to everyone, and the panic in the radio announcer's voices was evident.

I fidgeted as the morning's Scripture lessons were read. I

couldn't believe my ears. This was the passage, from ages past, chosen for this very morning:

God is our refuge and strength,
an ever-present help in trouble.
Therefore we will not fear, though the Earth give way
and the mountains fall into the heart of the sea,
Though its waters roar and foam,
and the mountains quake with their surging...
The LORD Almighty is with us.
Psalm 46

Whose "normal" do we live in, Lord? Why do unbelievable things keep happening to us? When we were hit with one more speed bump in this road we call life, I knew my only option was to turn to God, go to His Word, go to His people, be held, be hugged, and be assured.

Laugh and pray. That is our calling. For even the beauty of mountains can quake with surging and turn to ash, just like our quaking lives. But with God's touch and His care, He can turn the ashes to beauty once again.

10

just take me to jiffy lube

It took several years and then some, but the wildlife and flora slowly returned to the area around Mt. St. Helens. The same could be said for our lives, even after the news of infertility, then more cancer, then two unexpected adoptions. Our lives were starting to settle into a semblance of a routine, and we were enjoying the fruits of parenthood and occupation.

The post-eruption, local economy, like our lives and the landscape around Mt. St. Helens, slowly started to turn upward as well. While construction and logging work for Bill was slower to recover, business boomed for me. I became known as someone who had a gift for developing and implementing new occupational therapy programs, and had several lucrative opportunities to hone my gifting. Bill relished the chance to stay at home with his little girl. He showed Jamie what life was really like growing up on a farm full of pygmy goats, piglets, turkeys, hens, and birds.

Since we knew adventure was never far off, it came as little surprise when we were approached with the offer to transition from hospital work and home health to directing and implementing a new program in the emerging field of ergonomics and work-place wellness. I jumped at the chance.

We lived only a short five miles from the late 1800s building the owner of the company was buying and restoring. What treasures we found behind cabinets. I squealed with delight when we found an 1896 shoe button hook. Now I could show patients what a *real* button hook looked like!

We moved in and began working before the remodel job was done. The noise from the contractor's work was about to drive me crazy.

It had been a busy morning with meetings and patients. I had imperative dictation that needed to be completed for a legal deposition later in the day. It seemed that whenever I needed to focus and concentrate, the noise got louder. My voice was drowned out by buzz saws as I tried to tape the deposition. I did my best to hammer out my work, but the noise was becoming unbearable.

"I'm getting out of here," I told my secretary. "I'm going home where it is quiet so I can finish dictating this deposition."

I trampled heavily down the stairs to notify the contractor of the same.

"You're too noisy. I'm getting out of here." I sternly told him. "And I am not to be bothered with change orders until I return, y' hear?"

He looked at me and gave me a sheepish grin, then kissed me on my forehead.

"Sorry I'm so noisy, love. Drive carefully!"

What's a wife to do when the contractor is my husband?

As I drove home I realized just how nice it was outside. It would have been a perfect day to play hooky. The sun was shining. The skies were brilliant blue. And besides, it was Friday of Mother's Day weekend!

Almost arriving at our log home, I slowed the truck to a stop to let an oncoming car pass by. That's when I glanced in my rearview mirror and gasped with horror. The car coming behind me was definitely not slowing down. As it approached my stopped vehicle, I quickly tried to shift into gear and step on the gas. It was too late.

The impact was inevitable, and it was hard. I was thrust forward. My jaw hit the steering wheel, forcing my cheekbones into my eyes. The seat belt engaged and thrust me back into the back of the seat. I can still hear the crack as my head whipped back and was thrown hard into the rear truck window.

I watched as the other car rolled into the hay field across our drive. Still somewhat coherent, I jammed the truck into reverse and pulled into our driveway. I jumped out of the truck and yelled to the man in the other car, "Are you okay?"

"Yeah. I-only-havva-scratch, but-my-car is shtuck in the hay."

His words slurred together. It was only 10:30 a.m. but he was already drunker than a skunk. I made my way up to the house and dialed 911.

"What is your emergency?" I heard the voice on the other end say.

"I've been hit by a car," I said. My knees were beginning to wobble.

"Are you hurt?" the emergency operator asked.

"I, I . . ."

At that moment, my head seemed to explode and my back gave way. I dropped the phone, only to hear the operator say, "M'am? M'am? Are you there? I am sending help. Lie down and don't move."

As I laid there on the floor, I was scared out of my mind. My head was throbbing and my back was cramping. I had to do something. Instead of staying down, I hysterically hung up the phone and called my husband. Apparently I got enough information out to him that he not only jumped into his truck and sped home, he passed the emergency vehicles that were on their way!

I don't remember much after that, except for giving my social security number for my address and my phone number for my birth date. It was enough to confirm a head injury for sure!

My heart was broken. Our Mother's Day weekend bike trip was spoiled. Worse yet, our plans that we had just finalized three days prior, would be ruined. We had signed on with Compassionate Ministries to be on a long-term medical mission assignment in Africa. Tears trickled down my cheeks as the ambulance sped toward the hospital. Would someone be praying for me as they heard the siren wail? I sure hoped so.

I would spend a week in traction in the hospital and another six months at home in head, neck, and back traction from injuries sustained in the accident. The other car was going 50 miles per hour when it hit me. The impact and injuries forced my face to be rebuilt. It took years for the double vision to subside and the blood around the retina to be absorbed.

In the years to come, I would spend weeks and months in the hospital being treated by my peers in physical and occupational therapy. I had to regain function in both shoulders after they were rebuilt and remodeled. Today, both shoulders are held up, suspended by six lines of twenty-five pound test monofilament fishing line and anchor bolts. My back and my neck are screwed together at four different levels with nuts, bolts, washers, and discs, including a concoction of my own ground-up hip bone. The line blurs on where the DES related degenerative joint disease impact ends and the aftermath of the accident starts.

As independent as Bill and I are, we needed help. Jamie was six, and the unforeseen addition of Tim to our family happened in the middle of my multiple reconstructions from the accident. DES continued to ravage my body as well, leading to total knee replacements and revisions. Add one of the breast cancer surgeries and all this on the heels of the thyroid cancer surgery, and you have one busy season. But, as always, help arrived. It wasn't the way we expected it, but it was a blessing nonetheless.

Jamie and Tim raced into the house, slamming the front door shut with a swift backward kick of Jamie's foot. She clung to a box that was half her size. It had just been delivered by, "You know, Mom—that big brown truck!"

The kids were really good about not jumping or plopping on the bed where I hung in traction. They would stop about a foot from the bed, as they knew that even the slightest of movements could initiate excruciating pain, shooting from the top of my head to the tip of my toes. But excitement overtook any resemblance of carefulness. Jamie plopped the big box near my feet and jumped up on the bed. I took in an extra breath and did my best to disguise the pain from their wiggling and jiggling.

"Can we open it? Can we? Huh? Pretty please?"

They hardly stopped to take a breath between words. Their excitement was about to explode all over the bed.

"Puleezze, Mom?" they cried, their eyes wide and ablaze with wonder.

My curiosity was as great, if not greater, than theirs. I had wracked my brain over and over and couldn't figure out who was sending these packages to the kids.

"Oh . . . I supp . . . "

The ripping and tearing started before I could finish.

"It's another package from our Secret Pal!" Jamie squealed as she ripped at the wrapping paper and bubble wrap.

"Look, Tim! It's a gingerbread house that we get to put together!"

"AWESOME!" Tim said as he jumped up and down like a Mexican jumping bean, clasping his hands together.

As the kids annoyingly popped the bubble wrap, my thoughts tumbled over and over.

"Who could be doing this?" I wondered.

Whoever they were, they knew the way to Tim and Jamie's hearts, and they were speaking loud and clear to each of us by example. Their acts of love during this tough time of recovery and depleted finances helped to ease the pain and frustration the kids were clearly feeling. And the gifts just kept coming.

Every couple of weeks a letter or package would arrive from this Secret Someone. First came a month's worth of hot lunch tickets for school. It was an extra special treat—for me and the kids.

Next came the box of individual little boxes of cereal, fruit leathers, and boxed drinks. In it was a note:

"Here's for your happy mornings. Fix your own special

breakfast and don't forget to wipe the juice-staches off your lips!"

Another box was filled with cartoon lunch sacks, colorful napkins, juice boxes, cheese cracker combos, gummy fruits, and little boxes of cookies. It even came with individual candy kisses and hugs. The note this time:

"I know you fix your lunch most of the time, so have some fun and pack it fast! Angels are around you; remember you are very much loved. Hugs and kisses!"

Padded envelopes meant a special movie or kid's music tape. The kids would jump up and down when these arrived, and zipped through their afternoon chores so they could play the tape or movie as soon as possible. It helped the kids pass the hours that sometimes lingered long and hard.

Then, one day, a single long white envelope arrived. The letter inside:

> "I know how much you like to help out, and that you have done! You did great with breakfast, and had fun with lunch, so how about fixing dinner for Mom and Dad? With this letter, you get to 'fix' dinner. Just call the number below and ask for the manager. Tell them who you are. He is expecting you. The dinner is already paid for, and the pizza parlor will deliver it to your house. Figure out all the toppings that you want. They will also bring drinks, a tossed salad and ranch dressing, bread sticks and a dessert pizza, too! What you don't finish for dinner, you can pack in your lunch the next day! Don't forget to pour the milk and have napkins handy! Love, Your SP!"

This Secret Pal would write each child a note of encouragement every so often, laced with prayers and phone numbers of people they could call for extra help if they needed it. If they needed help with a carpool to soccer practice or swim team—call! If they knew Mom needed a grocery run and Dad would be getting home late—call! If they needed an extra hand with homework or with the laundry or other chores, or even if they just needed to talk—call!

Most of all, our kids knew they weren't doing life alone. They were surrounded with family and friends, known and unknown. It's a life lesson learned early, and not forgotten, even some twenty years later. I watch as they reach out to others in their time of need.

They go out of their way. They go the extra mile. They become the perfect stranger, willing to pick up a stranded co-worker and let them pour out their heart until the wee hours of a dawning day. They are the friend to the friendless, when everyone else has walked away.

Whoever the Secret Pal was, we still don't know. And that is how it will stay. But we still say prayers of thanks, and pass it on.

While we didn't know the kid's Secret Pal, several other "Un-secret Pals" helped us through some of our roughest times as well. There was Goon, a sweet 7-year-old boy who became my husband's shadow and wiggled his way into his heart. God knew the ache Bill had before Tim arrived. The balm was a young friendship bonded that words defy, even as Goon now has two boys of his own. His mom would become my chauffer and DQ

Blizzard Buddy. His dad, my medical guardian angel.

Then there was Dan and Louann Burns and their three ever-so-curly-haired, blond headed kids. A family who would be the answer to many of our prayers. They saw us through some of our best of times . . . and worst of times. They walked beside us through health crises, surgeries, adoptions, house fires, floods, and so much more. They introduced us to Clark's, the mom and pop hamburger joint that would become a favorite family tradition, especially the old-fashioned chocolate peanut butter milkshake with a banana split on top!

And then, of course, there was dear old Aunt Betty, the sister of my maternal grandmother. After Aunt Betty's husband of many long and happy years passed away, we worried about how she would get along without "her Johnny." He had been her all-in-all. Never much of a cook, they would eat meals out, favoring Grand Slams and Big Bob Burgers. How she lived through Uncle Johnny's frightful driving to meals is beyond comprehension. There is truth to the saying "never go faster than your guardian angel can fly." Apparently Uncle Johnny never got the memo!

After Uncle Johnny passed away, we pleaded with Aunt Betty to come live near us. We knew it would be best for her. But she would have none of it. Our concern grew as she became more and more isolated and alone. We tried every angle, to no avail. We chuckled as her concern for us, after the accident, was just as intense. We both worried long distance, calling and writing often.

"Finally," I said, beaming to my husband, "I think I know how we can get Aunt Betty up here! Let's ask her to come help me as I recuperate!"

I so desperately hoped it would be more of the opposite.

We were floored when Aunt Betty finally agreed. A two-month visit turned into a twelve year experience. And what adventures we had! We took her on her dream trip to Hawaii. We got her on a snow machine. And we even hoisted her into the hot tub, contorting every which way to get her five-foot-nothing frame in. We had to put a weight belt on her just to keep her from bobbing like a Halloween apple.

Aunt Betty did everything with us. She went camping and boating. She enjoyed activities with her great nieces and nephews and our special friends. Their kids became her kids, as she had never had children of her own.

Aunt Betty would entertain us with stories of being born in 1904, of living near Hollywood studios, and of riding in horse-drawn buggies or trolley cars. She reminisced about listening to radio for entertainment and being a flapper in the 1920s. She was proud of being a statistician, as it was called in her day, keeping the books in pencil, adding numerals in her head. Her accuracy stayed with her well into her 90s.

"Ewh! Ewh!" she would utter, as she waddled like a duck on ice, crossing a room. She lamented getting older as her sagging upper arms jiggled back and forth like Jell-O. "Aunt Betty Arms" my sister and I would call them, praying we would not share the family genes and inherit them. She never wanted to be 80 years old, nor 85, and especially not 90.

"I've seen enough in my lifetime!" she would say.

You can imagine what she said when she hit 95! And, even worse, you can imagine what I said when, in the midst of rehab from my ninety-second surgery, I realized my own Aunt Betty Arms had finally arrived. As I grunted and groaned, doing my physical therapy exercises in the mirror, tears began to stream down my face in pain. My triceps jiggled as I attempted to raise my unresponsive arm, and I bemoaned Aunt Betty's genes.

I stopped to let the jiggling subside, letting the tears continue to trickle down my face. Loving memories flooded my head, blessed for the years she and so many pals—secret or not—had helped us through many tough times. They each, in their own way, showered us with blessings and gifts of support, living out practical prayers . . . even if it meant driving me to Jiffy Lube to get re-built.

11

loss of a dream

While recovery from injuries, chronic health pain and surgery is hard, the grief and loss of our dream proved to be far more painful. For several years we had been preparing to work on the long-term foreign mission field. But the aftermath of the DES and repercussions from the car accident would change the course of our lives forever.

Given my regimen of doctor visits, surgeries, and physical and occupational therapy, it just wouldn't be possible to sustain a life overseas, especially in the areas in which we were focusing. So we resigned ourselves to the facts—we would have to stay put.

Jamie was devastated. She grieved the loss of an overseas adventure and seeing places she had only read about in books. She didn't think it was fair. She was mad at God. And admittedly, so was I.

One day, when Jamie and I were commiserating together, Bill sat us down. In only the way he could, Bill shared a valuable truth.

"Look, you two," he challenged us. "The call to the mission field never changed . . . just the place. And our place—*our* mission field—is always and only as far away as the end of our hands."

We looked at our hands, and then looked at each other. Without a word we slowly reached out and grasped each other's hands. That's when our family promised that we would never, ever forget: *our* mission field is only as far away as our hands. It's not just at church, but at the grocery store, at school, in the hospital, at doctor's appointments, or on a construction site.

Our normal continued on the Tuk pace. Never a dull moment. What would "at the end of our hands" *really* look like? It wasn't long before we saw it in action.

Jamie became involved in community service. Tim showed his gifting with computers and academic tutoring. Bill and I found that we had a niche reaching out to others walking through tough financial times, sharing tips on how to make it on a shoe-string budget.

We were able to walk with others who dealt with health crises. We kept our focus as a family. We carved out special time each week where all phones were off. All outside activities were cancelled. We spent time just as us—laughing, talking, sharing, and dreaming. We knew we needed each other. And we knew we needed God in the center. He would teach us. He would love us. He would show us where to go.

Sometimes our "at the end of our hands" was literal. Bill was known for being Mr. Tough Guy—the one to handle the skinned knees, adversity, and obstacles with panache. But Mr. Ninth in the Nation Heavyweight Wrestler, against his vehement assertion, was still human!

He found that out quite quickly when he found himself 180 feet high, on a concrete embankment, harnessed off, with a huge cable hurtling towards his face. There was no time to escape the evident. Even on tape, reviewed multiple times, it seemed impossible he would be able to avoid the speeding cable. Surely it would hit Bill directly on his head, and who knew what harm it would do. Unbelievably, at the last nano-second, instead of his head, the cable broke his left wrist and almost tore off his right thumb.

One hand in a cast, the other in a partial cast, how would Mr. Tough Guy cope? The days became his enemy. He had never experienced down time. He couldn't fill the hours with enough activity. To maintain the aerobic fitness needed for when he would return to work, Bill would often ride his bike around the town of Morton where we had moved to be closer to his job. This all happened when I was recuperating from one of my many surgeries. It included being hooked up to a chest-line IV five to six hours per day.

And oh, were *we* a sight to see!

One particular day, I had a clogged IV line. We headed to the clinic, four doors down from where we lived. The nurse stabilized the IV, but said we'd have to return in several hours when the doctor would be in. He would be able to clear the clot fully. As we left the office, we realized just how nice of a spring day it had become. Bill was antsy, and he could stand it no longer.

"Let's take the boat out for a spin while we wait!" He said with a pleading voice and a mischievous grin. The boat was our very first toy, the fruit of his union waged job.

"It'll keep our minds off of things!"

Against my better judgment, I agreed.

Just imagine the sight. Some guy with a cast on each arm and a woman with a chest IV. I carried the IV bag overhead while Bill put the Bayliner in the lake. He then hung the IV gently on the boat antenna. More than one person did a double-take.

The sun warmed our faces and lifted our spirits as we backed the boat down the ramp. The wind renewed our strength as we bounced across the lake. And all too soon, it seemed Bill was returning the boat to the dock.

We loaded up in ten short minutes and Bill dropped me off at the clinic.

"See you soon!" I said, kissing him on the cheek, thanking him for taking me *out* for lunch.

"If I'm not home, I'll be out riding my bike. Love ya!" He hollered as he sped away.

I got the IV line cleared in no time. My "fast-food lunch bag" and I took the short-cut home. As I emerged through the rose bushes, Bill came pedaling up on his mountain bike.

"Hey Lady! Goin' my way?!" he called.

"Why? You lookin' to give a hot mama a lift?" I teased.

"No, just your bag . . . lady!"

Once again, the tenets of faith, family, friends . . . *and fun* . . . kept our lives normal, even at the end of our literal hands. As we bounded down the streets of Morton, Bill with IV bag in hand and me chasing quickly behind, we couldn't help but wonder: Does Morton have a leash law?

Quite frankly, I think the Lord honored our diligence of seeking Him first. He gave us unique opportunities. Take Tobago for instance. (You know Tobago. That's where Disney filmed the classic *Swiss Family Robinson*.) Bill was given the opportunity to join twenty men from around the United States to travel to the tiny Caribbean island to help finish building a church.

Bill became endeared to the people and they to him. (Well, except the Voodoo queen and her daughters who didn't exactly like The Big White Evil One.) We have since had many wonderful trips back to visit our West Indies "family," joining in faith, taking part in worship, and often being the only "white men" in a sea of joyful black Tobagonian believers.

As God kept us on the move, the move was at times, a bit too fast-paced for me. Or, maybe I was the one going too fast. Either way, I found myself exhausted, needing a time of respite and renewal. I had nothing more to give to anyone—even myself.

A brochure arrived in the mail one day about a family retreat for those struggling through disability. I thought it would be just the ticket for our family. We could find hope and get a break from everyday challenges. It would be a time to learn, to grow, to be stretched, to network, to rest and renew, and to have fun in an environment joining others walking and living a similar journey.

We had been through so much with Tim and his challenges, not to mention my medical challenges and rehab. Plus, it would be at one of our favorite spots—Cannon Beach, Oregon!

Haystack Rock would loom on the horizon, the tidal waves would crash, surf flinging upward, the wind spraying pungent salt water on our faces.

Oh, I could already smell the famous freshly baked Haystack bread, its aroma filling the air as the golden white loaves came out of the brick oven. I could hardly wait to tell the family. Sadly, the response I received was not what I was expecting.

"You go, sweetheart," Bill responded. "Have fun, relax, and get renewed. But the kids and me? We need a break from disability. *I* need a week away from *anything* to do with disability. So, if you really want to go, have fun. Seriously. Go and have fun."

I struggled with Bill's firm decision, yet I understood. I knew life had been tough for all of us. But could I really go by myself? How could I go to a family retreat with no family? Oddly, something inside me nudged me to go . . . alone.

Several weeks later I found myself in Cannon Beach, not just to escape from my daily demands, but to attend one of the first Joni and Friends Family Retreats. Joni and Friends is the disability outreach of Joni Eareckson Tada, an internationally known advocate for the disabled, herself a quadriplegic since the age of 17.

As I made my way to the registration table, gulping down my last piece of Haystack bread, I heard a small voice inside me say: *You don't have to be here. You've seen Haystack Rock. You've breathed in the salt air. You've been to the bakery. You've been renewed! Run! Go back home!*

But it was too late.

"Welcome! My name is John!"

I was doomed. He pointed me to the check-in table, where

another chipper voice greeted me.

"What's your name?" the woman asked.

"Care. Care Tuk."

"*That's* your name?" she looked at me with a quizzical look.

"Yes," I said with a smile. I tried hard not to roll my eyes and sigh in exasperation, knowing what might be coming next.

"So where is your family?" she asked.

"I'm it for the week!" I tried to say cheerfully.

"Well," she huffed, the cheer clearly gone from her voice, "You *do* know this is for families or individuals affected by a *disability*, don't you?"

"Yes, I do . . . and I am."

"Well, you don't *look* like you have a disability."

AUGH! I wanted to scream. Just what does disability *look* like?

Here I was an occupational therapist, who not only worked with people affected by disability, I lived it. And so did our family. We lived it every day. I knew what disability looked like—even if it was hidden like mine.

I was coming close to heeding the advice of that small voice inside telling me to run. But my feet were glued to the floor. I realized this woman didn't know my story. She couldn't see my scars. She didn't know what our family lived out on a daily basis. I determined to stay.

The week was filled with fun, learning, growing, and networking with others. And I was glad I went. But it wasn't until the final night that my heart truly broke.

On the last night of the retreat, Joni gave a concert. As she sang, the words seared my heart. On one shoulder the "angel" was challenging me, saying: *Hello? Are you hearing the words?*

On the other shoulder the "other voice" was telling me to run. The volley inside my head continued long after Joni had finished the song.

My head throbbing, I made my way to the lobby. I looked around to see if anyone was watching. Then, I made a break for the door and ran. I jumped into my car and started driving. I was headed down Highway 101, in a heavy, cold, pelting rain with blustering winds. I was driving blindly, going nowhere in particular. I was just running from the voice I knew I needed to heed.

As the miles passed, panic crept in.

"What am I doing?" I screamed out.

Icy fear gripped me, realizing how dangerous it was for a single woman to be driving where she had no business being. It was a late coastal stormy night. I had no cell phone. I was a state away from anyone who knew me. It was ridiculous! I braked and made a U-turn on the deserted ocean highway. Through my tears I realized I couldn't run from God. He is everywhere, and He wanted more of my life.

It's not in trying, but in trusting.
It's not in running, but in resting.
It's not in wondering, but praying,
that we find the strength of the Lord.

The words of Joni's song rang in my ears. I knew what I was to do—I had figured that out earlier in the week. I was just scared. I was alone. And I had caved in to the smaller voice of fear. I knew the strength of the Lord was the only way I could do what was being asked of me. It's what "at the end of your hand" is all about.

I knew the truth. I still do. It is about being transparent and vulnerable enough to share the journey—filled with brokenness, grace, and mercy. It is a journey of believing God, not just believing in God. And as I rested more in Him . . . as I trusted Him fully . . . more opportunities came.

I had no idea that my little family retreat would ultimately lead me to being on staff at Joni and Friends. Eventually, I would hold the position of Assistant Director for . . . of all things . . . Family Retreats. But our family's biggest adventure would be helping to pioneer and develop Joni's program known as Wheels for the World. Working with volunteers, trucking companies, and even prisoners, the program helped collect, restore, and distribute previously owned wheelchairs and the gospel to individuals in need, especially in developing countries.

With my training as an occupational therapist and Bill's experience as a builder, we would go with Wheels for the World. Bill would be instrumental in designing and building a prototype wheelchair repair center for the local people in Ghana. I would learn to heed the advice of "avoid machine gun fire" in Albania. And we would serve the people of Russia.

While in Albania I would travel with our Joni and Friends COO, Doug, our photo journalist and media director, Mike, and our British counterparts from Through the Roof. Mike was quickly dubbed my "big brother" and we would end up experiencing a lot together.

As Mike and I watched over the city from our third-story, bombed-out lookout post, you couldn't stop from watching the local kids play their games of barefoot football. I could tell by the pained look on Mike's face that his heart ached for those kids. He knew the little urchins clamoring for coins and sorting through the trash looking for food were the same age as his grandkids back in the States. While the photo journalist in him nudged him to capture the moment in time on film, his ethics and solid integrity told him, not now. And when NBC Nightly News interviewed us, asking why we had come to Albania, we simply replied, "The need was greater than the risk."

The need was greater than the risk. As my artificial knees were knocking and my hands were visibly shaking, I knew that was exactly where the Lord wanted me.

As NBC Nightly News filmed, I settled down on the floor mat below me. Lutfa, a 40-year-old woman with severe cerebral palsy was placed in front of me. I rocked and swayed, working for over an hour to elicit some sort of relaxed tone in her rigid, crippled body. Therapy was unknown to her.

As I gently and carefully attempted to move her shoulder joint, I softly crooned a favorite tune of mine, the Sunday school chorus of Alleluia. Amazingly, I was able to slowly move her arm a slight three inches. Her aged mother began crying. It was more movement than they had ever seen in Lutfa.

I continued to croon "Alleluia." To my surprise, she started to croon with me, on key! Her brother, a local police captain, beamed and clapped. Her mother covered her mouth, stifling sobs. I continued. Then, I realized she was keeping time with me. I looked up to make eye contact with her mother, a devout Muslim, dressed in her traditional, cultural outfit, and saw tears stream down her face. Through an interpreter, I found out this was the first meaningful sound Lutfa had made in decades.

Mother to mother, our tears continued to stream down our faces. Soon Lutfa's tears joined ours.

Mother to mother, sister to sister, we were able to share our stories. As our time came to a close, we shared a hug that would last a lifetime. The wheelchair we found fit the police captain's sister perfectly. For the first time, Lutfa would be able to go outside her home. She could attend market. She could lift her eyes to the hills, from whence came her help. Holding hands we sang "Alleluia" one last time, letting freedom ring.

Only and always, at the end of your hand.

I would be remiss if I didn't include one last "at the end of your hand" story.

I never wanted cancer to be my thing—you know—my soapbox, my drama. But one day, a dear friend of mine, also a cancer survivor many times over said to me, "You know, Care, we who have survived cancer have an obligation. It is the honor and opportunity *as survivors* to help raise awareness, to talk about prevention, to honor those who have gone before us, and to encourage those who survive and walk beside us."

Talk about a whap upside the head. She was right. Marilyn got me to walk in my first American Cancer Society's Relay For Life® Survivor's Lap. I honored my comrades during the emotional Luminaria Lap. And I have never been the same since.

Ironically, I had worked with Dr. Gordy Klatt during my O.T. rotations. He started Relay For Life® to raise money for cancer research and treatment interventions. I had watched the news coverage of the very first Relay For Life® from my hospital bed some 60 miles away, recovering from my second breast cancer surgery. With tears streaming down my face I thought, "Wow. He's Relaying for me, and he doesn't even know it."

Since that first Survivor's Lap I've been involved on many levels—from local committees to working with our state legislators on insurance coverage. I had the opportunity to travel to Washington DC to speak with House and Senate members relating to cancer. I said to them as I say to you right now:

"Stop what you are doing. Look to your left. Now, look to your right. Realize that one of you will be affected by cancer in your lifetime, and we can change that."

It's all at the end of your hand.

12

no regrets

It had been an incredible mid-May day—an unusually warm spring for South Central Alaska. Granted, our warm is much different from those in the Lower 48. Highs of 50s or 60s and we have a full-fledged heat wave! Nothing is better than Alaska in springtime.

The peas were popping up their tiny heads. The spinach leaf lines were uniform and seemed to grow as I watched. The long Alaska days serve to grow things faster and bigger. And in the spring, every gardener is dreaming of growing the elusive State Fair record. (Last year a cabbage weighed in at 90 pounds!)

I was refreshed from a day filled with dirt and digging. I never take lightly the fact that I could actually kneel on bionic knees to pull the wild asparagus and horsetail weeds. I took pleasure as I felt the sun on my back and let the warm soil sift through my fingers. I had transplanted a dozen or so of the volunteer pansies that had wiggled their way up through the driveway gravel. I was grateful I felt reasonably little pain, especially since the last surgery was only 5 weeks prior. I actually had a day of doing and feeling "normal."

As I fell into bed, sweet sleep overtook me quickly.

I awoke Sunday morning unable to move. I tried to roll over. Every muscle screamed out.

"AUGH!" I growled.

Another "Body Betrayal" morning.

Am I overdone from yesterday? I thought to myself. *Probably.*

I groaned as I tried to move my bionic legs, willing them to flop over the bed.

I reached for my water glass next to the bed and murmur under my breath, "Lord, why after actually feeling normal for one of the first times in forever, do I have to feel so crummy today? Will I ever have a time that I can count on being normal two days in a row?"

Letting my legs dangle from the edge of the bed, I knew the best medicine would be to reach for my daily devotional book. Tears slipped down my cheek as I read the words. I could nearly hear God's tender voice whisper back to me as I read from A. J. Russells book, *God Calling:*

"How unseeing the world as it goes on! How unknowing it is of your heartaches, your troubles, your battles won, your conquests, your difficulties. But be thankful that there is One who knows, One who marks every crisis, every effort, and every heartache."

"Thank You, Lord." I whispered back. "I'm sorry that I gripe and whine, especially when today it is more of my own doing, in my longing to be normal. I overdid it, not stopping to think or pace myself. Thank you for being patient with me when I long to be normal, knowing full well my normal will be unlike

122

anyone else's. But you have made me new with bionic parts and pieces. You have made me able to function as I never thought I could. I am so blessed that you know what I am going through, even on these tough days. Thank you for never giving up on me."

As I opened the bedroom door, the smell of cranberry and banana scones greeted me. I slowly limped across the room.

"G'morning, gimp! Do a little too much yesterday?" My loving husband chuckled and gave me a hug.

You don't have to be "bionic" to have body betrayal. We all have days we do too much, not stopping when we know our limits. After all, we want to be normal. We want to have fun. We want to be like others.

As the Good Book says, "Pride goes before the fall . . ."

I wish I could say I've learned my lesson. I wish I could tell you that I am better about pacing myself these days. It's not as if I set out to sabotage myself. I just get caught up and excited for the day. Then, before I know it, poof! I've gone over the line. Now I'm cranky and tired. My knees are so swollen they look like cantaloupes. My swollen hands look like baseball mitts. The left side of my face droops, losing the wrinkles on my forehead—a real sign I'm toast and something I can't hide from my husband or family. I'm caught!

Finding a balance in daily life is difficult, especially when our married motto is "no regrets." Long ago we learned that today is the only day on which we can count. Tomorrow is just a vision. And yesterday is a distant memory.

People who live for tomorrow die wishing. People who live for yesterday die discouraged. People who live for today have no regrets, for they are living the very moment.

So Bill and I have purposed to focus on today—the right now. I suppose part of that comes from my dad; something he gave me when I was only eight years old. I still remember as if it were yesterday . . . .

There I was, sitting in the church pew, trying my best to keep my wiggle bottom still. I folded my white gloved hands as neatly as an eight year old can in her uncomfortably starched church dress lap. I skooched a little closer to my dad as he opened the Episcopal Church's Book of Common Prayer. The priest began to read the passage for that Thanksgiving Day. The selection was Matthew 6:25-34, but the main focus was on verses 33 and 34.

My dad leaned over and whispered in my ear, "This is my favorite passage in the *whole* Bible, ever since I was your age. Never ever forget it. It will serve you well in life."

I listened, mesmerized. I'm sure my little mouth was hanging a bit open.

"Therefore I tell you, do not worry about your life, what you will eat or drink; or about your body, what you will wear. Is not life more important than food, and the body more important than clothes? Look at the birds of the air; they do not sow or reap or store away in barns, and yet your heavenly Father feeds them. Are you not much more valuable than they? Who of you by worrying can add a single hour to his life?

And why do you worry about clothes? See how the lilies of the field grow. They do not labor or spin. Yet I tell you that not even Solomon in all his splendor was dressed like one of these. If that is how God clothes the grass of the field, which is here today and tomorrow is thrown into the fire, will He not much more clothe you, O you of little faith? So do not worry, saying, "What shall we eat?" or "What shall we drink?" or "What shall we wear?" For the pagans run after all these things, and your heavenly Father knows that you need them. But seek first his kingdom and his righteousness, and all these things will be given to you as well. Therefore do not worry about tomorrow, for tomorrow will worry about itself. Each day has enough trouble of its own."

Fast forward nine years. I was a high school senior, preparing for graduation. I was filled with all the fear and trepidation that goes with stepping out into an unknown future. My mom's death had turned my world upside down and backward. Nonetheless, I was carrying on the best I could. Cramming for finals, my dad would pop his head in as I studied, "Don't forget to Matthew 6 it!"

On graduation day, Dad slipped in as I was adjusting my cap and gown. Tears welled up in his eyes as he handed me a card. It was only the second time in my life I had seen my dad cry. The first was the night my mother died. I had been the only one home when he got back from the hospital. He had collapsed in my lap, tears streaming down his face and guttural sobs wracking his six foot, five frame. The graduation card did not have my name on it, only "Matthew 6:25-34."

No words had to be spoken. We just hugged each other tightly, letting our tears flow and sobs fill the room.

This scene was to be repeated 14 years later. Dad lay hovering in and out of a coma. The last goodbyes had been said by most of the family. Now it was my turn. Every so often Dad would break out of the coma and be lucid.

During one of his clear moments he motioned me over, grabbed my hand, and said: "I need you to do me a favor and let me do this my way. I need you to leave. Drive home and be with Bill and the kids. Go home for me . . . please? Don't worry, I'm in good hands. And Care? Remember Matthew 6:33."

I was caught a little off guard.

"But Dad," I replied, "I thought you said the important verse was 34—don't worry about tomorrow?"

"No," he said quietly, "It's 33. Now get outta here and call me when you get home."

At that he lapsed back into a coma.

Tears streaming down my face, I kissed him, gave his hand a squeeze, and headed home.

"Thirty-three or thirty-four" I whispered all the way home. Pulling up the driveway, my husband met me with a strong knowing embrace.

Between sobs I told Bill, "I have to read something really quick. I'll be right back!"

I ran into my bedroom, grabbed my Bible, and looked up Matthew 6. I vaguely heard the phone ring in the other room as I read. And once again, Father did know best. It was verse 33. For if you pursue verse 33 (seek first His kingdom), verse 34 will follow (you won't worry about tomorrow).

As the reality sunk in, Bill rushed in and motioned for me to hurry and answer the phone. I didn't need to. I already knew. I looked up and smiled.

"You are in good hands, Dad!"

Mom and Dad had taught me the importance of faith, of seeking God first in my life, in making right choices, and knowing that all things would work out—some way, somehow. They showed me, by the way they lived, that actions speak louder than words. Dad especially taught me that by taking one day at a time, and living in the moment, you could truly have no regrets. My dad was spot on with something else as well: tomorrow has enough troubles of its own. My life is living proof of that.

Bill's parents emulated much the same. They didn't wait for retirement or their "golden years" to venture out. Weekends would find them camping, fishing, and exploring areas near and far. Their days as dairy farmers and milk trucking were filled with long hours of hard labor. Yet they turned it into a family affair, spending quality time together working hard, but finding time to play hard as well.

"No regrets," Dad would say, talking about being fire captain of the local volunteer fire department.

"No regrets," Bill's mom would recount, chuckling as she told the story of burying her beloved third child, Gladys, in her raucous leopard spotted undergarments.

"She was, after all, the wild child of the family," a smile greeting a slipped teardrop.

Because Mom and Dad showed us a bigger world, we knew a bigger world. And so would their grandkids.

Bill and I pray Jamie and Tim continue the adventure. We

pray they remember their time in Tobago, scuba-diving, and moving to Alaska with fondness. They have had the chance to learn how to snow machine, how to stay on an inner-tube while Dad drove the boat, and how to remodel every home they would ever live in. They have had the opportunity to work in a soup kitchen and sing in *Psalty's Singing Songbook*. They had the chance to do big things.

We know they, too, have no regrets, even when there are consequences for the choices they make. What more could we ask for?

Our families knew life. They knew loss. They knew hard knocks. But most of all, they lived and taught Bill and me to live each day with no regrets—no wishing for a do-over. That didn't mean our families were Pollyanna, pie-in-the-sky, types. Rather, they were realists. Bill's family would struggle with anger toward the driver who killed their daughter. But they also knew good would come out of it. For today, someone sees because Gladys' eyes were donated.

Our little family has had to work our way through our own issues as well. We know we have struggled with denial, unrealistic hope, and bargaining with God. We have had to work through times of despondency and anger, and the agonizing question, "Why us?"

The resounding answer: "Why *not* you, good and faithful ones?"

Sure, it pains me to know that our kids grew up thinking normal involved Mom being sick or recovering from some surgery. I would be lying if I didn't say that I struggled knowing that would be their normal.

There were days I would whine. There were days I would

complain. But then it would hit me. I not only had an amazing family, wonderful friends, and unshakable faith; I had fun. I had the priceless peace that passes all understanding. I had been given the precious gem of life. I had riches untold in more ways than ten! I had gifts that allowed me to walk out my new normal. I had titanium rods, plates, and screws. (My "inner bling.") I had gratitude to literally be able to walk out each new day. I am encouraged every morning, for, even if I have over-done it, I awake to another day to believe, and have no regrets.

We all have times we struggle with our faith. We howl: "How can we possibly hang on? Are you there, God? Is anyone home? Are you listening?"

But the question lies within us. Will those who watch us on a daily basis find us truly faithful. Through thick and thin, good and bad, as we struggle and walk through 90-plus surgeries, through chemo-therapy, through daily searing, unrelenting pain, fatigue beyond measure, and financial turmoil.

We are found faithful when we are real. We are found faithful when we are honest about the pain and the struggle. We are found faithful when we reach out to someone else we see walking the same journey and encourage them. We are found faithful by putting one foot in front of the other and moving forward.

We are found faithful by God and others because we have made a choice to be faithful. We choose our attitude of gratitude. We can be in pain or we can be a pain. We are found faithful by finding something to do "at the end of our hands"—

by making right choices and taking one day at a time. We are found faithful by living Matthew 6:25-34, but especially verses 33 and 34.

Faithful with faith. Faithful with family. Faithful with friends. And faithfully having fun as we live each day with no regrets.

13

sentence of silence

Rich Indian summer colors adorned the landscape of the tiny town of Elk, Washington. We had moved to Elk in 1994, this time following a rural home health and school O.T. position. It was the end of August, which meant harvest was in full swing. Second cuttings of hay were baled, potatoes were dug, and corn was picked. Crisp apples were being pressed into cider, dried into slices, or canned as applesauce or pie filling.

Then there were the cucumbers—ready to brine for Grandma's crunchy bread and butter pickles or Bill's famous dills. Oh! Don't forget the box of Yakima peaches! If I don't make my lazy day cobbler, then they'll be ready to can for sweet winter treats. I was in heaven, up to my armpits in canning and cooking.

While I know the true meaning of Labor Day, around our house it meant a totally different kind of labor—constant! And by the looks of it, Labor Day 2001 looked to be the granddaddy of all Labor Day marathons. Peaches, apples, cucumbers, corn, jalapeño peppers, green beans, peas, pears, and more were lined up in boxes, ready for the processing mania.

Jars had been sterilized, crocks were ready for the vinegar

brines, jar rings and lids were stacked in a fashion that made it easy for Bill and me to grab and go. Bill's mom's famous canner—graciously passed on to us—sat proudly upon our 1952 wood-electric Monarch stove, waiting for its annual contribution for our winter sustenance.

We were elated when we found out my husband would have not just a three-day holiday weekend, but four! An extra day built into a canning marathon meant we could maybe even slow the pace a bit and enjoy the time! We jumped in with both feet.

I began preparing the cucumbers, getting them into their brine so they would be ready to go once my husband got home. But deep down, I knew something wasn't right.

Due to a minor diaphragm palsy earlier that year after one of my shoulder surgeries, I had to have weekly oxygen levels taken. It was a short, in and out reading, much like taking your blood pressure, but it had to be done in the doctor's office. As I evaluated my schedule and thought through everything that needed to be done that weekend, I knew I had just enough time to get my oxygen level taken and be back in time to start the pickling processing. Yet of course, in typical Tuk fashion, things did not go as planned.

When getting my level taken, I mentioned to the doctor that I had been dealing with a funny headache over the prior two days. I chalked it up to the dry weather, smoke from area grass fire burns, and of course, getting ready for the canning marathon.

The doctor asked, "Is it like a sinus headache?"

"No. And I'm not snuffleupagusing, either," explaining our family phrase for nasal congestion.

"A migraine?" he queried.

"No way!" I retorted. I knew what *those* felt like.

"When do you notice the headache?" he asked.

"Only when I bend over, like brushing my teeth or picking something up off the floor."

"No questions asked young lady," he replied. "You are going to get an x-ray NOW!"

I pleaded with him, explaining I didn't have time for an x-ray. I had pickles ready for canning. Besides, it wasn't that big of a deal.

"I shouldn't have said anything," I said to myself.

"Humor me, and get going NOW!" he said again, letting a small smile break through past his lips.

Reluctantly, I followed his instructions.

What happened next neither of us was prepared for. As we reviewed the x-ray, I saw a round object over my temporal lobe.

"What is *that*? It isn't a tumor. Is it an air bubble or a brain burp?" I asked.

With a chuckle he assured me you cannot detect brain burps on an x-ray.

"I'm not sure what it is, but I do know that it means you are headed immediately for a CT scan. I have called the techs. They are waiting for you."

No amount of persuading, arguing, or pleading could dissuade him.

Not only was there no discussion, there would be no canning for me. Not that weekend, not the next, nor the rest of the season. In fact, I did not return home for two months.

We quickly learned that the "burp" on the scan was a three compartment, subdural brain bleed—*in my brain!* One compartment was probably an old bleed. The second was semi-active. The third was a full, all-out active bleed. The pressure in my brain was so great that the left hemisphere was pushing into the right. I was rushed from the x-ray department to the main hospital. In less than 24 hours I was on the operating table, fully entrenched in brain surgery.

Suddenly Intensive Care had a whole new meaning . . . and Bill got to do the canning!

The saying says that "paybacks are hell." Now, while I don't use the "h-e-double-toothpicks" word that often, there are times the saying is appropriate. One of those rare occasions was after my surgery. I had finally stabilized and was moved to a local rehab facility.

I had lost my ability to walk, talk, or perform basic daily living activities. I was imprisoned—not just in a foreign body—but in a foreign living situation. The Traumatic Brain Injury floor was filled to capacity. I was stuck on the Stroke Ward, and most people were 30 to 40 years my senior. My room was directly across from the extremely busy and noisy nurses' station. And quite frankly, I figured I might as well be in h-e-double . . . .

I was non-verbal. That meant I knew what was being said and for the most part understood it, but I couldn't verbally respond. So when the 9-11 terrorist attack on the Twin Towers happened during my second week at the rehab facility, you can imagine the commotion. The confusion and emotion circulating around 9-11 had residents and staff equally on edge. Every radio—every television was on. I found myself very despondent and sinking into depression. My head was throbbing.

I had been an occupational therapist for over 25 years. As a therapist, when I worked with a person who had a brain injury, one of the first things I did was ensure they would be in an area of little distraction. I knew the brain was working overtime to heal and rewire connections that were lost or damaged. Being in a calm, quiet environment with low levels of commotion helped to decrease agitation, disorientation, or confusion. No such luck for me.

Peace and quiet were virtually impossible, especially with the 9-11 commotion. On top of it all, I was worried about my nephew and his family who lived and worked in the financial district of New York City, but of course, I could communicate it to no one.

If that wasn't enough, my roommate proved to be a challenge as well. By the time I arrived she had already been in the hospital for two months, recovering from a stroke. Within two minutes of my arrival, she saw the cross on my wedding band and made it extremely clear that no talk of religion, God, or prayer would be allowed in our room. She vehemently stated that she was a firm atheist.

I sank back on my bed and dissolved into tears. Silently, I cried out to God, "I can't do this!"

I could hear Him chuckle to me and say, "Well, now that *that* is taken care of, we can go forward. I can show you how I can work in spite of it all."

"Yeah right, God," I silently mumbled back, crocodile tears cascading down my face.

My pity party was interrupted with a nurse summoning me to afternoon small group physical therapy. They wheeled me down and put me in a circle with 20 other people. (*This was a small group?*) It was one more assault on my personal O.T. senses.

My entire right side did not work. I was sentenced to silence. I could not tell anyone when I was in pain or when my surgically stapled head felt like it was going to burst. Here I was—an active, athletic 47-year-old woman confined to silence. I wasn't nursing home bound. I was a wife and mother of two. And I *had* to get back to the canning!

Suddenly, the group of senior citizens began chuckling. As I did my best to figure out what they were laughing at, another woman close to my age was wheeled in.

I couldn't believe what I saw. Tammy, the wife of the local university football coach, seemed to be my spitting image. We both had shaved heads. We both had gnarly scars on our heads. We both wore the same popular brand of athletic shorts, and both wore t-shirts of the same color. Even our brand and type of socks matched. We both wore long leg orthotics and our tennis shoes were not only the same brand, but the same color and size! Tammy could talk, and I could not. But we immediately knew we would get to be friends.

And friends we were. We spent our free time in her room, which was much quieter than mine. She had been blessed with a "VIP suite" due to her husband's standing in the community. While we got to know each other, we discovered we were both women of faith, and we both agreed that this was a true "Godcidence." Our friendship is the only thing that got us through the 9-11 attacks.

One evening when sitting on Tammy's bed, the youth pastor from her church playfully burst into the room wearing a "Bob the Tomato" VeggieTales™ t-shirt. He then broke out into song—nothing less than "Where's My Hairbrush" by the one and only Larry, the talking cucumber from VeggieTales™. We laughed as he regaled us with the entire song. But as we listened to the words, we were actually quite impressed with the personal implications.

The point of the Larry Boy song was that poor Larry was looking desperately for his hairbrush, not realizing that he, a cucumber, had no hair. Quite poignant for two bald women.

Tammy and I made a pact that once we were out of rehab, we would meet together and purchase Larry Boy t-shirts in celebration of our friendship and victory in our roller coaster ride through cancer, brain surgery, and complications. We set the date for March 16, 2002. (My husband and I were set to move to Alaska on Friday, March 17.)

On Monday, March 13, I confirmed our date through a note to Tammy via her husband. He assured me that Tammy had read the note and would be out of the hospital by then. We were set.

As I was doing some final packing on Wednesday, March 15, my husband called me into the living room. Emphatically he told me to sit down. I didn't understand at first. Then, I saw it. Streaming at the bottom of the television screen was an announcement that our beloved Tammy had lost her battle with cancer.

I sat stunned. Who would be there to "know" what I've been through? Who would my partner in rehab mischief be? Tears trickled down my cheeks.

On March 16, 2002, I bought my Larry Boy t-shirt. I also bought a Larry Boy plush stuffed toy. Today, Larry Boy sits

on my desk, adorned with a pin that says "no whining"—
something Tammy and I pledged we would try hard not to do,
no matter what happened to either of us nor how hard things
got. I still wear my Larry Boy t-shirt, especially on days when I
need to "hear" Tammy's encouragement.

As I battle cancer again, sporting a bald, Army-issued-
type hairdo from chemo, I sing to the heavens: "Where is my
hairbrush, O where is my hairbrush?"

I can hear Tammy singing with me, and both she and God
are chuckling.

When I began to regain my speech after the brain bleed, it
wasn't exactly an overnight occurrence. For someone who has
no problem using each and every word linguists say women
have in a given day, not being able to verbalize correctly what
I wanted to say irritated me to no end. I can't imagine what it
must have been like for my family and friends, especially my
incredibly patient husband. (Although I can only imagine he
enjoyed the peace and quiet!)

Hindsight what it is, my speech had probably been on its
way out prior to the actual subdural bleed. To this day, the
physicians are not sure what caused the bleed. As with many
things with me, they just chalk it up to "Care-Tuk-it-is."

Most subdural bleeds are from a blow to the head or a fall.
I'm part of the .004 percent of "unknown origins." Nevertheless,
we did realize that we had been playing "charades" a great deal
leading up to the bleed, willing my mouth to do what my family
implored: "Just spit it out!"

My brain was in continual word-search mode. And when I couldn't find a word, I tried to act it out, as in charades. My speech therapist said it helped that I was in the medical profession, as I utilize the top 10 percent higher functioning parts of my cerebral cortex to retrieve information I needed to treat my patients. (I wonder if she was just trying to make me feel good.) She explained that my brain "fast-forwarded," acting like a thesaurus, searching for the word before I would spit it out. Often times I would be unsuccessful.

Even today, when I get tired or over-stimulated, I fall back into the word-search/charades mode. How my husband can figure what I mean to say baffles me.

Then, sometimes, my syllables get transposed. I have trouble with blended syllables like "bl" or "sl". Try living in Alaska and one of the thirty or so words I never got back is "slamon" (aka: salmon). My husband delights in trying to get me to say aluminum. I usually get so frustrated I blurt out "FOIL!" Otherwise, it comes out "nimulimanum" or any conglomeration you can conjure up.

The harder I try, the worser (yes, another word that didn't come back) it gets. Don't try to get me to "condenstrate" as it's like trying to "quesense" the "ablaphet"—you know, the A, B, X, D ,F,C's? Truly, I can see the alphabet in my brain. But I cannot say it, let alone try and put it in order. And when I'm really having a bad day, I even type what I speak! I pity my recipients when they get one of those emails. They must think I am speaking and typing in tongues!

Another post brain injury speech challenge I had was my speech would sometimes get garbled. Not in the typical stroke type sense. Instead, my word patterns would, and do, become confused. Speech therapists characterized it as "object-subject-verb" word order. If you were to ask me, "How are you today, Care?" you would expect me to say, "I'm okay, how are you?" But what you would get, if you're lucky, is something like, "Okay be mine are. Fine it be you?" (I'm not joking!)

I got used to speaking that way. So did my family, my speech therapist, and others. If you didn't know me, you would be baffled. But stick around for thirty minutes on a bad day and you will start speaking just like me! My physician's staff said it took them an hour or so after I left an appointment before they quit talking like me. One of my friends dubbed it Yoda Speak! And quite frankly, I don't mind. In many ways, I identify with Yoda.

Besides Yoda being of "unknown origin" (who *is* or *what is* a Care Tuk anyway?), I love his warrior spirit. He is filled with wisdom and discernment. I love his ability to discern the light and dark side of a person. Yoda speaks very much from his heart, and is a consummate encourager.

He is a teacher, a leader, yet ever humble and never seeking the limelight. He is firm in his counsel to younger Jedi to "train yourself to let go of everything you fear." While all of the above features are ones I hope others might see in me, it is Yoda's speech that makes the two of us, beyond a shadow of a doubt, kindred spirits.

14

dreams under the midnight sun

The brain bleed happened just as Bill and I had become true empty-nesters. Tim was away at college in Iowa and Jamie was married and living in Alaska. As I struggled through recovery, we made the difficult decision not to have the kids fly home. I needed a stable, quiet environment in which to recover.

We were also afraid that the shock of what I looked and acted like might be too much for them. After all they had been through with me over the years, this time Bill and I felt we needed to do this just the two of us.

During my recovery, Bill and I shared many tender moments. We would recount the many blessings of our "no regrets" journeys and kingdom capers. We talked about our "dream list"—the list of things we hoped to do or places to visit in our lifetime. The only one that hadn't been ticked off was moving to Alaska.

Oh, it wasn't that we hadn't had the opportunities. We had turned down four separate offers due to various seasons of obstacles or adversity. We knew that the outcome of the brain bleed had taken my career as an occupational therapist away and that I would have to go on disability. We knew not what tomorrow would hold realistically for me. And many tears wet the pillows at night . . . for both of us.

That's when one night Bill shot up off his pillow and said to me, "That's it! We're gone! We are outta here!"

And gone we were, against our better judgment and that of the medical professionals (they didn't feel I was stable yet, my speech had not come back, and I still had motor coordination difficulties and visual/perceptual losses to deal with.) In three short weeks Bill quit his job, put our house on the market, packed us up lock, stock, and barrel, and we were off.

He had no job waiting for him, but he "knew what he knew"—that God had never failed us yet and that He wasn't about to. If anything was going to happen to me, Bill knew he needed to be by our little girl, Jamie, who was already living her daddy's dream in Alaska. (Tim would find his way up to Alaska seven years later, much to all our delight.)

To this day we are convinced that it was the best decision we have ever made. Many people didn't understand our move at the time. They thought we had rocks, not just loose screws, in our heads. In retrospect they have come to see that Bill and I belong in Alaska. When people ask Bill if he is native (Alaskan) he replies, "Yep! It just took my body 45 years to get here!"

And oh, the adventures we've had up here.

I don't take it lightly that I actually get to live on my dream property. To watch moose, fox, or bear trample through our yard is exhilarating—and scary—all at once. And I wouldn't trade it for the world.

When in corporate leadership trainings years ago, an exercise they would have us do would be to draw our "dream place." Mine always included a creek or river, trees, a cabin, and mountains ... and sun! While I believe that dreams can *and do* come true, I didn't think this one ever would—especially in Alaska!

Nevertheless, when Bill moved us up to Alaska he got back in touch with a college buddy of his. We spent many long hours out at his cabin, enjoying BBQs, Sunday Italian spaghetti feeds, fishing, playing bocce ball, and getting reacquainted after 30 years. I would spend most of my time down by the river, fishing line in the water, practicing the art of patience. Truly, it didn't matter if I hooked anything or not, but if I did, good luck pulling me from the river's edge.

We were living with our daughter at the time, spending the summer looking for just the right piece of property. We made offers on several places, however none of them materialized. Our friend kept encouraging us to buy 20 acres of his that he had for sale. It was just two parcels away from his cabin. At first, we didn't think he was serious. Yet, Dave kept after us. We didn't want to take advantage of the friendship, and we knew that until our house in Washington sold we really couldn't even consider his offer.

One day, while down at the river on the 20 acres he was encouraging us to buy, he and Bill sat and watched me. Fifteen minutes went by ... thirty minutes ... an hour ... two hours. Finally his buddy piped up, "You know, Bill, I can see Care someday walking along this river with her walker. We'll all be in our nineties. She'll be studying the river, hollering to us, 'Hey fellas! The Kings are in!' You know this property is just what she needs to help her recover."

Bill had to agree. He had never seen me so at peace—so content—especially at one of the hardest times in my life. My speech was slowly returning. My balance was still iffy, and I was coming to accept that I would never practice as a clinical occupational therapist again. I didn't know anyone except for Bill's friend, my physician, and my own occupational and physical therapists. For someone who was a social network queen, this was pure anguish.

We talked about our friend's offer again that night before we went to bed. Against every fiber in our logical being, we decided to take a leap of faith. Despite our house not selling, we took Dave up on his offer. We started the real estate ball rolling.

Wouldn't you know it, but within three days time, we got a call from good friends who were living in Hawaii at the time, asking if our place in Washington had sold yet. They were interested in buying it as they were making a move back stateside. As I said before, there are no coincidences, only Godcidences!

That, my friend, is how Care's Corner came into being. For God knows, there is peace by the river—peace that passes all understanding, goes beyond all comprehension, and fills our inner being to its fullest, until we, pressed down, and peace overflowing, can turn around and offer the same contagious peace and be a blessing to someone else.

Life in Alaska would prove to be a true adventure. We would build our little piece of heaven on that 20 acre plot. We would share our dream with friends and relatives from around the world. And we . . . ourselves . . . would be blessed along with way.

◆　◆　◆

"Let's go!"

"Go where?" I said.

"We're going!" she said.

"Going where?" I repeated.

"I'm paying!" she replied.

"Paying for what?" I asked.

"This!" she pointed to a sign, "C'mon! Let's hurry. We have no time!" she said in her broken Dutch-English accent.

My husband's cousin from Holland (whom I claim as my own, thank you!) was in Alaska for a visit. Her daughter and son-in-law were driving the Anchorage/Fairbanks loop, camping at Denali and points along the way. But Henny wanted to stay behind to spend time with us. We hadn't seen each other in over 15 years, and we had a lot of catching up to do.

It was a glorious May day, but I was still feeling bad. I knew Henny would only be in Alaska for a short time and not get a chance to see the famous Denali. So, on a whim, one morning I decided that she and I would pack a picnic and go up to Talkeetna where we could at least give her a taste of Alaska and, with a little luck, see Mt. McKinley. As we wound through Willow, there was Denali, in all her glory. I have never heard such a litany of delight spoken in Dutch.

We had a grand time in Talkeetna—wandering through the town, eating at the café, touring the local historical museum, spending "girl time," and relishing every minute. As the day was coming to a close, I knew we needed to head back home to fix dinner. But suddenly, Henny poked me and said, "Let's go!"

145

That's how the bantering began. She was talking about flying around Denali!

Only in my wildest dreams had I ever thought I would get to experience such an adventure. Something like this was surely not in our medically depleted budget. But Henny was determined.

She went to the ticket counter and began asking questions. She quickly learned that there would be no more single flights going that day, but we could tag along with a couple from New Zealand. Unfortunately, the flight would be the more expensive two and a half hour flight as it would include a landing at base camp on Ruth Glacier, some 14,000 feet in elevation. I knew we could not afford that, but Henny was insistent. She was adamant that we would somehow take the flight. She would not take "no" for an answer.

I finally ushered my cousin to the side and told her to let me do the talking. (Not that I had any clue what I was going to say.) I returned to the counter, explained I was a local resident, and showed her my driver's license. I also explained that the reason my cousin did not join her daughter in the Denali excursion was because of me, and that I was just recovering from my recent "bionic" leg repair, as well as cancer.

The receptionist finally took me aside, out of earshot of the New Zealanders who were paying full fare, and said, "Since you are local, and since you will be doing public relations for us for the rest of the summer, we will give you half fare. Is that acceptable?"

Is that acceptable? I nearly choked.

In mere minutes we were being instructed on where survival gear could be found, our headsets were adjusted and we were

squeezed into a little five-seat plane (the fifth seat was more of
a cubby hole where my cousin opted to be.) I had just enough
time to call my husband and ask, "Honey, is it okay if we are
a bit late getting dinner on the table? We have a chance to fly
around *and land* on Denali."

I could hear every bit of jealous restraint in his voice as he
graciously said, "See ya when you get home, dirt bag (one of
our terms of endearment)! Seriously, have fun! You do have the
camera, don't you?"

Of course, I never thought to put my camera in the bag.
After all, flying to Denali was never on my radar. As the plane's
prop was being manually started, I ran to the mercantile
and grabbed two disposable cameras—just enough film to
document the flight.

There will never, ever, in an entire lifetime of books or
stories, be enough words or paint to fully share what we
experienced. How do you put into words the depths of ice
crevasses, watching with awe as the climbing groups made
ascents on the summit . . . seeing Anchorage from afar . . . the
sight and color of true blue ice . . . moose, bear, and the tundra. I
was so close that I was sure I could touch Heaven.

I can't come up with a better excuse for being late to dinner,
can you?

I didn't think so!

So, we thought we had arrived in Heaven . . . or as close as we
could get to it and still be on good old Mother Earth. Life was
running relatively calm, finally! I dared to believe that we had

arrived at some semblance of normal.

Yet it was only the calm before more storms.

15

seriously . . . again?

It was the start of a new year. January 2003. I had just slipped out of bed and was preparing for the day. As I bent over to put my shoes on, I heard a loud pop. Immediately, I knew it wasn't good. (Not often are loud pops from your back a good thing.) Turns out, I had ruptured two discs in my back. The ravages of the DES degenerative joint disease were back, and I knew it wouldn't be pretty.

The side-effects of DES had plagued me throughout my life. Off and on, it would show its ugly side. Eventually, there was no choice but to fuse my back and neck in four places. It would require four surgeries. The knees, not wanting to be left out, one day decided to crumble, literally.

Because I was a "complex case," Alaskan doctors felt it would be better for me to be treated by the experts in the Lower 48. They were, after all, the surgeons who had been keeping my Humpty Dumpty body together with nuts, bolts, and screws over the last 40 years. The care was first-rate, but the itinerary was draining.

Every three months for five years I would need to fly "Outside" (what we Alaskans call the Lower 48). It was killing our finances, and it was a drain on my body. Quite frankly, it was a drain on our steadfast faith. I was used to being up and active and I wondered if it were ever to be again.

I would continue to wonder, especially as the pain in my back, hip, and legs grew worse, if I was on the mend or if something more serious was lurking on the horizon. Eventually, I would succumb to using my walker. Falls were a regular part of my daily routine.

My appetite for my husband's wonderful cooking waned and I began to lose weight. You would think losing weight would be most women's delight. Normally, it would have been. But I had just reached my lifetime goal, a feat long worked for. And now, pound by pound, I was slipping beneath that goal.

The doctors were mystified. Yes, I was anemic, but not enough to be extremely concerned. Iron supplements would be prescribed. And the waiting game began.

That's when I felt a lump near my hip. At various appointments with multiple specialists they all agreed—my digestive system must just be slowed down by the iron. When I kept pushing, and the pain was becoming unbearable, it was decided that I should go to the Lower 48 for a check of my back and leg hardware to make sure nothing was wrong there. It wasn't.

To make matters worse, I contracted the H1N1 virus while away in Seattle. Go figure. If anyone could get it, it would be me. There I was, stuck. Unable to fly because of extreme congestion and coughing, I would have to look for housing on the outside. I cringed when several of our good friends offered to house me. I knew they would be put at risk of getting the virus (and unfortunately, a couple did).

I was blessed with the calm peace that pervaded the homes of the friends with which I stayed. It allowed me time of solitude and contentment. They knew me well enough that often I needed to go to the sea to breathe. So, wrapped in the warmth of a hand sewn quilt that over the years has earned me the loving nickname "Ma Squaw," they piled me in the car.

Ah, what a time to be able to relax along the Pacific Ocean. It was precious time in front of a crackling fire. I soaked up every moment as I walked along the beach and sat on the sun-bleached logs. It allowed me time to reconcile the "pulls and tugs" in my life.

I was slowly on the viral mend. But there was still pain in my lower right quadrant.

Once home, the unbearable pain landed me in the hospital. After several miscues attributed to my past medical history and being that infamous "complex case," it was discovered that the lump I was feeling in my right lower abdomen was most likely a tumor. It would require surgery.

With my medical background, it wasn't rocket science when I reviewed the CT scans with the surgeon. I knew. "It" was back . . . again.

As I drove home from the appointment, my head reeled.

"Seriously, God? Again?" I whispered.

Yep. Seriously. Again.

Soon Bill and I would learn it was stage 3+ colon cancer that had me in such pain and anguish. We would be in an office with a Hawaiian shirt clad oncologist in minus 10 degree weather asking us, "Well guys, how are we going to do this?"

It wouldn't be like all the other brushes and battles with cancer where surgery would get it all. This time, I'd add a new twist.

Chemo.

During chemo, I joined an elite group that enjoys a camaraderie that many hope not ever to know. You get to know people in a different way. You measure the progress of your treatment by the amount of hair loss (or eyebrows or eyelashes). You can tell what kind of week they have had by the color of their skin. Is it jaundice yellow? Is it pale and accompanied by sunken cheeks and black circles under their eyes?

You can tell how they feel by how many blankets they request from the warmer, or how tightly wrapped they are in their own fleece blankets that they bring. You know not to ask questions when they bury themselves under the blankets, their nose and mouth barely visible. You often times hear people joke about the "molting season" they are in, as the skin on their hands and feet peel, layer after layer, week after week.

Conversely, there are those who are chatty, whose nausea is under control, or possibly who have found a chemo cocktail that agrees with their system. It may be a good week for them or maybe they are on a maintenance dose of medication—possibly on the hopeful side of remission of this ugly disease.

In remission. Out of remission. Tumor markers look great. Tumor markers have risen. Blood levels are good. Blood levels have tanked. Transfusions. Infusions. Injections. Rejections. It is a white knuckle roller coaster ride. It is like being on a carnival ride that does not discriminate against age, height, weight, color of skin, ethnicity, heritage, gender, religious preference, political alliance, hair color, length or lack thereof.

There are no rules.

Yet—like the Big Top—it takes all kinds, shapes, and colors to pull off the "Greatest Show on Earth." And the "Greatest Show on Earth" is life itself.

Life is colored by people of all heritages, all lines of work, all social strata, all ethnicities, all ages, and all genders. Just like in life, in chemo you are thrown into the melting pot. Like any good recipe, a sourpuss attitude can ruin the whole batch, just as much as a bright personality with just the right seasoning of humor, friendliness, and levity will make the chemo go down a bit easier.

So, we raise our hands high when we are at the top of our treatment, possibly in remission, possibly just having a good day. On those days when the bottom drops out from underneath us, we know we have a cadre of new friends who will buoy us up, because they have been there . . . because they care . . . because they know.

They remind me that I too can make it through, just as they have. We are each in our seats, belts and IV's hooked tight, ready or not to go at it one more time . . . until that time that we can get off the white knuckle ride, and climb back on the merry-go-round of "regular" everyday life.

And so the chemo went—slow and steady with regular bouts of nausea.

My new, yet again, normal.

As I drift between dreamland and the new day ahead, my nose twitches. Somewhere in the post-chemo cobwebs I hear a kathumping. It's the sound of my loving husband filling the wood box for the chilly Alaska day ahead. I roll over and groan.

My eyes still shut in rebellion, cobwebs from the restless night tangle with each other. As I fight the morning, a winding trail of smoke creeps into the bedroom window, cracked open ever so slightly. Its scent, acting as its own alarm clock, tickle my nose into a grand announcement with a loud "AhhhhCHOO!"

A second announcement follows. The noise resembling a fog horn as I blow my nose. Ignoring the morning smoke signal prodding, I hunker down further under the layers of sheets and comfy blankets. I do my best to disregard the snooze buttons, denying it is time to get up. An hour later, I finally feel semi-awake, at least enough to face the day.

I am normally a "side sleeper," pillow between my legs. Yet somehow, during my fitful night of little rest, I ended up on my back. Awakening, I feel like a beached whale, hardly able to move. My hands feel like well padded catcher's mitts. I struggle to open and close my hands. My left arm, feeling like lead, in some way ended up at a 90 degree angle over my ski-hat covered head. My wedding ring is held hostage on a finger that is double its normal size.

Gazing at the time on the alarm clock, I know the inevitable. I have to get up. Arthur (aka: arthritis) has clearly set up camp in my fused spinal column and neck. My anchor bolt and fishing line laced up shoulders slump heavily. My knees and legs, with their state of the art, prototype configurations of metal and hardware, are barking in protest. Willing my limbs to work in concert, I attempt a log roll, planting my elbow on the bed's edge, rolling as one, swinging my legs over the edge.

Seated upright, my brain works overtime to jolt my foggy short-term memory. I find myself begging my brain to remember the basic tasks of the day ahead.

I take a shot at standing up. The first three attempts end with my backside plopping back on the bed. Success at last, I take a stab at stepping out to make my way to the bathroom. I feebly take my first steps. My calves let their complaints be known, accentuated by groans of "ooch" and "ouch."

"Death on a cracker sounds pretty good to me right now," I mutter to the mosquito, with its irritating buzzing in my ear.

Brushing my teeth, I look in the mirror.

"Who is *that*?"

The person I see does not resemble the person I thought I would see. The person I so longingly hope to see in the mirror is only an intellectual and deteriorated figment of my imagination. The bald head makes the weight loss that shows in my face even more accentuated.

"Why, oh why, are mornings so hard?" I sigh.

What used to take a blink of an eye to be up, showered, dressed, and ready, now takes laborious and intentionally focused time. I plop a denture tablet into a water-filled container and place my retainers in the water. They are the retainers that keep my jaw in line after having my face rebuilt.

Knowing I must keep the hustle going, I grasp the grab bars on the wall and carefully lift my legs into the shower. I sit on the built in shower seat, hanging onto the hand-held showerhead, waiting for the water to warm up. I chuckle when I think of guests comments of the many adaptations we have made in our home. Grab bars by the shower. Raised (18") toilet seat. Raised woodstove. Raised refrigerator. Raised washer and dryer.

As an occupational therapist, never did I think there would be a day that I would think "therapist: heal thyself!" I now know my former patients' frustration with sock aides, reachers, or orthotics. Gone are the days of "zip, trip, and out of here!"

Finally, almost two hours later, I grab the car keys, a pillow on which to prop my arms, and the walker (just in case). I'm off! It's a day I know will set me back for two, but that is the price I choose to pay.

The day will include the usual reason to go to town—doctor appointments and a stop to get my chemo port flushed. I will attempt a bit of grocery shopping. It's a task that brings a great deal of neurological stimulation . . . often too much.

I never thought that scanning row after row would be so difficult. Since the bleed and chemo, my vision is impacted, as are my perceptual abilities. Combine the two, add a lot of people jostling around, and it spells trouble. I find myself in the same trouble when I attend any event—from large churches to movies or parties where there is high stimulation. Even a fast paced television show can spell disaster! I close my eyes and ask my husband, "Is it done yet? Can I open them yet?"

I treat myself at the end of the day by meeting friends for coffee. They stand to give me a light hug and say, "Wow, you look so good!"

Oh, if they only knew.

16

looking back

I lay in the hospital bed, recovering from a "two-fer" day that turned into a "two-fer" week. Getting my strength and stamina back after chemo has been hard. My body was only able to tolerate half the amount of chemotherapy first thought possible. My body became too toxic. The side effects were so brutal that the doctors, and my family, made the difficult decision to stop treatment.

My blood counts and tumor markers continue to fluctuate, putting me in and out of remission. The rollercoaster continues. For now, we are opting to let God be God and go for quality versus quantity. As you can imagine, it was a tough decision.

Gazing out the window, I lazily watch a young male eagle take flight. He is one of five eagles which call Care's Corner home. As the wind whips across the hay field, he soars on a blast of cold Arctic air. His majestic mottled colors of black, white, and brown glisten as sunlight reflects through his pin feathers. It won't be long until he will be sporting a body of midnight black and a stark white head.

My mouth falls open in awe.

He glides against the backdrop of the snow-covered

Government Peak and the Talkeetna Mountain Range.

I take a deep breath and slowly let it out.

I wonder what that young eagle thinks about as he soars higher and higher until he is out of my sight. Does he wonder what tomorrow will bring? And where are the other eagles, the rest of his family or his other feathered friends?

I settle back in bed, the young eagle gone for now. Try as I might to get some rest, my eyes are drawn back to the window, straining to catch any sign of another eagle soaring on the wind-swept sky.

Walking through eleven bouts with cancer, this last time with the added complexity of chemo, I have been buffeted with challenges that have made each step of my daily life much like bucking heavy headwinds. No soaring like an eagle. No catching a warm thermal that would send me to higher heights.

My health—once more out of my direct control—has landed me back into a sentence of silence. I've been set aside, away from my normal routine. I'm tucked quietly away at home, kept from the outside world and from doing what I like best. For now, no working out. No laps at the pool. No book club—bantering opinions between colleagues and friends. No more fellowship at church.

I even have to tell my two kids that as much as I miss them, and as much as I want them to drop by, my immune system is too compromised. They both work in highly public places and the risk is too great that they might carry stray germs that are lethal to me right now.

I am learning that this sentence of silence is another time to "be still and know"—a time to T.R.U.S.T. (Totally Rely Upon the Savior's Timing). It is time to R.E.S.T. (Relinquish

Everything and Submit Totally). I didn't see this at first. It actually felt like this sentence of silence was more like solitary confinement.

While friends and family did their best to encourage me, as my sentence dragged on, communication sharply declined. The phone calls, emails, and notes of encouragement seemed to drop off. I *knew* that it didn't mean they didn't care. I *knew* it meant that people were consumed with their own daily activities.

It was the basic truth lived out—out of sight, out of mind. Yet head knowledge and heart feeling are two different things.

Some would say if they were hurled into a sentence of silence they would assuredly slip into a state of depression. Many who are confined to isolation naturally hurtle into tears, loneliness, or even despair. I've even heard friends say that desperate times bring desperate measures.

For me, desperate times bring me to the end of myself. Desperate times—in my times of silence—bring me to my bionic knees. I am humbled to see what is really important, and often it has little to do with me.

I would be dishonest to say that sometimes my seasons of silence have not brought me to tears. I have known days gripped by the icy tendrils of abject loneliness. But when I have cried all the tears there are to cry, and when I have etched out every bit of loneliness, I find—at the end of myself—a sweet peace. It is a release that I believe can only be brought by the One who has walked this road before, the One who truly knows.

Out of the corner of my eyes I see the young eagle reappear.

Watching him, I realize that as he flies, he has a choice. He can be buffeted by the 50 mile per hour winds that are howling across his face, or he can adjust his wings ever so slightly and soar to heights he has never imagined. He can rise higher and higher, as he wings his way back to his nest on Care's Corner.

As I crane my neck, watching him soar out of sight once again, I sink back on the hospital bed that sits snuggly up against the picture window, framing the vast Talkeetna Mountains glowing in the Arctic sunlight.

I let my breath out and smile from deep within.

I finally recognize my sentence of silence—my season of stillness—is allowing me to soar to heights never imagined. Right here, in the depths of quietness, coming to the end of myself, on my back, I look up. Oh, the places I can go . . . right from here.

The kids were over tonight to celebrate my birthday. It was a day I wasn't sure I'd make it to. We enjoyed a great time of laughter, and we feasted on Bill's scrumptious culinary delicacies. The family surprised me with a gift of a professional photography session with the family at Care's Corner, planned for this weekend, just as the fall colors are popping out in all their glory. I pray the forecasters are correct and the weekend actually will be sunny!

As I crawled into bed, I smile. As I drifted off to sleep, my thoughts begin to bounce all over the place. I wonder if I will be here to celebrate my next birthday. I wonder if I will get to see this book actually in print. I wonder if the kids and Bill gave me

this gift not because they knew I truly *wanted* a family photo—
since the three of them hate having their pictures taken—but
rather because it would be the last memento of us as a family
together at Care's Corner.

Those thoughts are real. They are . . . I think . . . in the mind
of every cancer survivor at some point. It isn't fear. It is reality.

Then again, I remind myself, I could hit a moose on the road
and meet my Maker tomorrow. Any of us, for that matter, could
go tomorrow. None of us know.

My brain continues to bounce. Sleep eludes me. I quietly get
up and fix a cup of Beth's Friendship Tea in my new Cannon
Beach mug. The puffins on the side are smiling back at me.

Sitting in front of the glowing woodstove, wrapped in the
prayer shawl lovingly stitched and sent to keep me covered
during chemo, my mind runs through a maze of other people—
people I call my Heroes of Hope. They have journeyed with
me over the years. They are the ones who have stood by my
side through thick and thin. Though they think I have a few
loose screws upstairs (besides the cranial screw that really is
loose), they are the ones who have been there to bandage up my
inevitable skinned knees.

These heroes are people who inspire me. They affirm me.
They pray for me and stretch me. They calm me down . . .
whatever the time of day or night I might call . . . wherever in
the world they may be. They not only listen, they point me to
the One who can do something about the situation.

They have opened their hearts and homes to me. They have
shuttled me back and forth to appointments. They have learned
the inside intricacies of occupational and physical therapy as
I stayed at their homes for weeks, sometimes months on end,

recuperating from my litany of surgeries. They have adapted their bathrooms with grab-bars and raised toilet seats, recliners and sofas were remodeled so that I could easily get up and down.

These bearers of hope could be in Spokane or South Africa, Enumclaw or Elk. They might be in Rock Valley or live on Rainbow Lane. My call tonight might go to Beaverton or Bothell, Camano Island or Centralia/Chehalis. Lemons come from California and funny cards from Fargo. "Care" packages arrive from New York, Wenatchee and Washington, DC. Maxine cartoons arrive from Tennessee and Tacoma. Welcome words ring from Wasilla.

I can't imagine going through life or walking this journey without them. I do not have to speak their names. They know who they are and the special place they hold without a word.

It didn't matter that they might be going through trials or troubles of their own. They were there for me. They loved me enough to kick me in the keister when I needed it. They cared enough to cry with me. They were concerned enough to cry with me. They shared lessons they had learned, hoping in turn that I would find encouragement.

These Heroes of Hope have shared personal lumps of coal, harshly mined and turned into treasure through their own battles with cancer—their own unique struggles. They themselves are diamonds, living through the pain and produce of death. They have faced the tragic death of a loved one or the ache of a wayward child.

But most of all, my Heroes of Hope endured with me. I just pray that maybe . . . just maybe . . . they, too, have been blessed by all we have shared and walked through together.

Am I ready to leave this mortal life? You bet! In fact, on some days I find myself more than ready. And on some days I'm actually quite perplexed as to why He has yet to take me—unless He figures He's not ready for me to foul up Heaven. Or, maybe . . . just maybe . . . there are more adventures and opportunities He has just waiting for me to experience.

I am weary. I am worn. But, I am willing.

I am willing to walk down a road I would rather not go—whether that be surgery, chemo, rehab, or just day-to-day. I am even willing to be financially challenged, or be set apart from whatever normal might be. But I know I can do it because of those around me—those on "Team Tuk."

Even though they might not even know me, they know my challenge. They know my struggles. They know the pain. They encourage us. They laugh with us. They cry with us. They pray with and for us. They remind us daily that we can do one more round, and that they will be there by our sides. They hold our weary arms up. They stand in the gap for us. They help us as we "count the cost"—which is much more than a financial cost.

As I step one foot in front of the other, whether it's on days like today when I am weary, or on days when I am worn, I pray that I will be found faithful. I pray that I will be found faithful by you, the reader, and by those I meet as I walk through this medical maze. I pray that people will find me "walking my talk" and making right choices.

I pray I will be found faithful by those who walk beside me, by those who come behind me, and by those I might never even meet face to face. But most importantly, I pray I will be found faithful by the One who calls me by my name.

I pray that I will be willing . . . no matter what.

afterword
until we meet again

You know, if I hadn't lived this life, I'm not sure I would believe this crazy story. I'm not even sure Ripley would believe it. Some people ask me if I am in the Guinness Book of World Records for numbers of surgeries yet. I smile and reply, "Not yet, but I am aiming for 100!"

The road has been long. No, let me re-phrase that. The road *is* long! And I know I'm not done yet. Maybe . . . just maybe . . . that's the point of all of this.

For my story is your story.

We have all skinned our knees at some point. We have all had days when we have felt off our rocker, like we have a couple loose screws in our heads. There are just a few of us who actually do have a cranial screw or two that are loose.

Our stories will continue long after we are gone. Our siblings will tattle on us. Our sons, daughters, nieces, and nephews will tell their kids about us.

My prayer is that this book has brought you hope for the journey on which you are walking. I pray that you know you are never, ever walking alone. You have brothers and sisters . . . and a Heavenly Father . . . who care about you. Yep, plain ol' you!

165

Just like me . . . plain ol' Carolyn Jane.

I hope that you have laughed with me and at me. I'm used to it. As I've shared my stories of loose screws and skinned knees, I trust you have been able to, in some small way, relate.

I hope that you will remember to look at your hands daily and ask yourself: "What can I do today, at the end of my hand?"

For you truly do make a difference.

I hope you will take the time to grab your Bible and look up Matthew 6:25-34. Use it as a reminder that things will work out—especially if you "33 and 34" it.

Your life matters and things will work out.

I hope that I might have given you a window into the life of someone who has a disability—whether you can see it or not. And if you happen to be facing an illness or disability, I pray you see it as an opportunity to face your challenges, share your obstacles, overcome your adversities, and turn them into an adventure of a lifetime.

I hope you remember to take time for you. Don't become selfish, but instead be realistic. Find your Care's Corner—that little spot you can go to be still, to know, to listen, to be refreshed, and to be renewed.

Don't forget to look up while you are there. The eagle may be soaring overhead, taking your soul on the thermals up to the heavens. Yet another day for adventuring—even through adversity and obstacles.

Most of all, I hope you, too, will grab hold of the tenets of faith, family, friends . . . and fun. And don't forget to dream a little. After all, they do come true, even under the midnight sun.

See you soon!

until we meet again

loose screws & skinned knees

resources

Joni And Friends

Joni and Friends was established in 1979 by Joni Eareckson Tada, who at 17 was injured in a diving accident, leaving her a quadriplegic. Since its inception, Joni and Friends has been dedicated to extending the love and message of Christ to people who are affected by disability.

Joni and Friends is committed to recruiting, training, and motivating new generations of people with disabilities to become leaders in their churches and communities.

www.joniandfriends.org

Relay For Life®

America Cancer Society Relay For Life® is a life-changing event that gives everyone in communities across the globe a chance to celebrate the lives of people who have battled cancer, remember loved ones lost, and fight back against the disease.

www.relayforlife.org

Young Life

Introducing adolescents to Jesus Christ and helping them grow in their faith.

www.younglife.org

Casting for Recovery®

A national 501(c)(3) non-profit organization supporting breast cancer survivors through a program that combines fly-fishing, counseling, and medical information to build a focus on

wellness instead of illness.
www.castingforrecovery.org

AnGeL Ministries

AnGeL Ministries is the independent, non-profit organization of Anne Graham Lotz based in Raleigh, North Carolina. They are committed to giving out messages of Biblical exposition so that God's Word is personal and relevant to ordinary people.
www.annegrahamlotz.com

Midnight Sun Oncology

Midnight Sun Oncology provides exceptional, personalized care for people with cancer and blood disorders.
www.midnightsunoncology.com

Educare Consulting

Clinics provide diagnosis, consultation and/or counseling to help the dyslexic and family of the dyslexic understand their difficulties and differences in the way they learn.
deedeecurran@educareconsulting.com

Luis Palau Association

Proclaiming the Good News of Jesus Christ to millions of people each year through city-wide evangelistic campaigns.
www.palau.org

about the author

Care Tuk is a nationally known speaker, educator, and retreat/workshop leader. She has been a school, hospital, and home health occupational therapist for more than 30 years. She has been named as a Top Business Woman in America and recognized for her work with youth, disability outreach and awareness, and the American Cancer Society.

Care lives in Wasilla, Alaska with her husband Bill. They have two grown children, Jamie and Tim, who live nearby.

At the time this book went to print, Care had completed treatment for her eleventh bout with cancer.

loose screws & skinned knees